Tom Roberts

"Go forward, dear"

A horseman's life and legacy

written for Horse SA by
Dr Andrew McLean
& Nicki Stuart

Published by Horse SA

www.horsesa.asn.au

Woodside, South Australia

ISBN 978 0 9945721 3 4 (paperback)

ISBN 978 0 9945721 4 1 (e-book)

Design & layout by Penny Stewart & Annette Sheedy

Printed by Ingram Spark, Australia

Contents

The Science of Training; Movement Needs; Social Needs;
Grazing Needs; Clarity in Communication Needs; Mental Abilities;
Learning; Negative Reinforcement; Positive Reinforcement;
Punishment; Classical Conditioning and Lightness; Habituation;
Shaping; Cues and Signals; Self Carriage; Short Sessions and
Rests; Flight Response; Arousal and Fear.

Foreword

This is a book that needed to be written. What a tragedy if the life and work of Tom Roberts had been lost and forgotten over time.

Thanks to Nicki and Andrew for the research they have done to produce this work.

Robbie influenced so many horse-men and women over the years, a friend to so many, and most importantly, a friend to the horse. I have never known two people with such enthusiasm and energy as Robbie and Pat and I wonder how many of us realised at the time what a treasure we had.

My hope is that future generations will read this book, carefully, and take note of his wise words.

It is with great affection and gratitude I have penned these few words to the memory of Robbie, a remarkable man and a truly great horseman, and I think how lucky I was to have known him.

Erica Taylor

Introduction

In sitting down to write this, I reflect on the hours of support and advice provided by Pat Roberts to both Horse SA and to me personally. Pat emphasized to all the value of continuous education for riders and owners to improve the overall welfare of horses. She always encouraged Horse SA to keep building the equestrian knowledge base, on several occasions suggesting I needed to 'write more!'.

Many hours were spent having cups of tea at her Richmond residence, the small kitchen table full of newsletters from the myriad of horse and donkey organisations she supported and was a member of, right until her last days. The talk was always about Tom and his work and profoundly, the need to keep striving for horse access onto public land, and the ongoing advocacy work to ensure horses remain a valued part of our Australian community and culture.

It was a surprise when, after her funeral, a member of Pat's family made contact seeking a suitable home for Tom's famous bit collection and a few other items from his lecture-writing room. With the help of some supporters, we loaded several boxes of gifted items into a horse float for transportation to storage. A parting word from a family member noted it was Pat's wish that education for horse owners be continued.

Fortunately, many who knew Tom and Pat had this vision too, including the Horse SA Management Committee, Dr Andrew McLean and Nicki Stuart, who agreed to shape a rough idea into the eloquent tribute you read today. The work could not have proceeded without the help of valued sponsors and volunteers.

This book now serves as a tribute to Tom Roberts, the man and his messages underpinning 'timely, thoughtful horsemanship' and a more ethical way of training.

Funds raised from book sales will go towards future projects to preserve elements of Tom's work, enabling the sharing of knowledge with the next generation of riders.

Horse SA, through members, volunteers and supporters, continues work to advocate for horses to remain an important part of our Australian society, to access public land and to provide educational opportunities. Tom and Pat influenced the South Australian horse community to an extent we are only just beginning to appreciate. Ultimately, it is the horse who is the beneficiary.

Julie Fiedler
Executive Officer, Horse SA
www.horsesa.asn.au
www.tomroberts.net.au

Preface

A great part of Tom Roberts' legacy is the goodwill his name engenders among the Australian horse community. That cohort is aging; we are hopeful this book will bring Tom's important work to a new generation. The memories of his students and friends, so graciously and lovingly shared, added depth and dimension beyond the primary resources.

The impetus for this book came from a desire to preserve the films shot of Tom at work with horses by his wife, Pat, before they are lost to the passage of time. At time of publication this is an aim yet to be realised, but we trust that these important archives will be saved for all to share. Pat bequeathed a portion of the vast collection of written material and artefacts she and Tom collected to South Australia's state horse owners' advocacy group, Horse SA, for preservation and display.

The exceptional organisational skills and drive of Julie Fiedler (Horse SA's Executive Officer) ensured this book became a reality, as a means of raising funds to manage the Roberts' collection. Thanks go to the volunteers Julie corralled to assist with archiving and collation.

Practical assistance in compiling material and photographs was provided by Carol Neller, Caroline Payne and her daughter Jessie Rae Preece.

We are also grateful for the insightful and supportive editorial assistance of Dr Portland Jones and the proof-reading of Dr Robyn Stokes – both busy professionals who donated their time to this work.

Tom and Pat's family generously passed on precious memorabilia, photos and documents that without which, this book would not have progressed beyond a 'nice idea'. We spent many hours sifting through Tom's four 'Horse Control' books, re-visiting and re-discovering the many thoughtful facets of his approach to life and horses. When quotes in the following book are unattributed this is where we have drawn from the text of Tom's books and his personal writings. They are his voice.

We thank all mentioned here and also our loved ones who supported our endeavours and endured our preoccupation with a man and his horses.

Dr Andrew McLean & Nicki Stuart

About the Authors

Andrew McLean

PhD (Equine Cognition & Learning), BSc (Zoology), Dip Ed

Researcher and Coach, Equitation Science International, Andrew is widely considered one of the leading academic experts on horse training. He is a winner of Australia's highest science award, the Eureka Science Prize and in 2013 won the John H Daniels Fellowship to the USA sporting library and was instrumental in forming the International Society for Equitation Science, for which he is an Honorary Fellow. Andrew has written 5 books on horse training and co-authored 40 papers in scientific journals. In 1989, Andrew won Australia's premier Horse Trials, the Gawler Three Day Event, and represented Australia in Horse Trials that year. In 1990 he was short-listed for the World Championships in Stockholm. In Dressage he has competed to FEI level and trained horses to Grand Prix and he has trained and ridden to Grand Prix in Show-jumping. He has also held a race trainer's licence and has ridden in bareback races in Australia and New Zealand. He has coached some of the world's greatest riders, coaches and trainers and reformed internationally competitive horses up to Olympic Games and World Championship level, as well as some top Australian racehorses. Andrew is most widely known for his work in behaviour modification in sport horses and his development of the Australian Equine Behaviour Centre. In addition to training horses, Andrew has also developed successful foundation training programmes for working elephants, now implemented in Nepal, India, Thailand and

Myanmar through his co-founded charity foundation, Human Elephant Learning Programs (H-ELP). Andrew's training has been heavily influenced by Tom Roberts through his books and through his contact with Pat Roberts in the later years of her life. Tom's approach resonated with Andrew and he recognised the significance, both practically and historically of Tom's knowledge of the psychology of horse training.

 **Nicki Stuart** is a journalist, trainer of horses and riders, and practitioner of Equitation Science. She currently owns and manages Kersbrook Equestrian Centre in the Adelaide Hills, after a 20-year career with the Australian Broadcasting Corporation. Her first exposure to Tom Roberts was as a high school student during her studies for her Year 12 certificate. Tom's 'Horse Control' books were required reading for the 'Horsemasters' course and students were tasked with breaking in their own mount. Nicki recalls referring, as many have before her and since, to 'The Young Horse' as a guiding text. Her exposure, also, to Maurice Wright, author of 'The Jeffery Method', instilled a lasting way of thinking about horse behaviour and training. Later in life Nicki met Andrew McLean and their ensuing friendship and professional collaboration adds a unique depth to this book. Nicki likes to think that if Tom were able to sit on the sidelines of her arena and observe her starting a young horse or helping a horse onto a float, he'd recognise his legacy in her approach; and indeed, in the practices of all contemporary trainers who use the philosophy of 'profit you, profit you not' to seek the best learning outcomes for their horses.

Tom (left) on Mr & Mrs Norm Thomas' grey 'Winston' and Capt JJ Pearce (right) on Miss Dorothy Mansom's 'Elkedra'.

Tom in the Adelaide Park Lands, 1977.

Part 1

Tom Roberts, the Horseman

by Nicki Stuart

Tom Roberts.

Chapter 1

From Little Things

What are the qualities people are describing, when they say that someone was 'before their time'? Mostly it's said after they're dead and, as the world catches up, hindsight reveals just how forward thinking they were in their theory or methods. Occasionally, it's said of those who stand out in their own lifetime.

Thomas Alexander Roberts, 'Robbie' to his friends, was a man shaped by his time, a man of his time, and it could be argued that his methods will be useful for all time. That's a pretty big 'wrap'! If you're reading this and you knew Robbie, it will come as no surprise; "it's justified", you'll say. If you've only just discovered Tom Roberts, the horseman and his teachings, you'll soon appreciate why.

Horse-keeping South Australians had the most extensive exposure to Tom and his principles by virtue of his decision to take repatriation from England to Australia after World War I. His direct influence in this State on generations of mostly amateur horse riders and trainers was greatest through the decades directly before, and those after, World War II. Tom's reach, however, was not limited to South Australia; it was both national and international, especially after the publication of his series of 'Horse Control' books.

The Australian horseman Tom Roberts may well lay claim to being the most popular 'horsey' author in the world; certainly the letters keep flooding in from all parts of the globe from satisfied readers of his Horse Control series.

'Hacking About', *The Horse Magazine*, September 1987

These volumes were soon recognised for their contribution to horse training and welfare. They set a new standard for clear, horse friendly methodology which was accessible to all.

Tom Roberts' method was to find out all he could about the history and behaviour of the horse. Then he would think deeply as to what could be the cause of the unsatisfactory behaviour. Next he would work out a practical corrective programme that could bring success. His method of approach and his solutions can surely be employed in widely differing cases. Every thinking horseman will be a better equipped horse master after reading this book.

Miss Kay Irving B.A, M.B.E, reviewing Tom's final book, 'Reminiscences', for the *Hoofs & Horns* magazine, October 1984. Tom and Kay formed a friendship through the Australian Pony Club movement.

The books were the culmination of Tom's life work with horses, a life that neatly spanned most of the 20th century. An extraordinary century on so many fronts and, for the horse, the relationship with humans that evolved thousands of years prior was impacted irreversibly by the rise of motorised transport and farm machinery. When the horse was at risk of becoming redundant, humanity's sentimental view of the species and enjoyment of sporting pursuits ensured its re-purpose and survival in the roles for which it is now most familiar; that of companion animal, entertainer and athlete. None, of course, for which an individual horse volunteers, and thus the onus falls onto those who keep and train them to do their best by the animal. As Tom states:

"If you are fond of a horse and wish to do him a real favour – train him well. Teach him good manners, good habits, both in the stable and under the saddle. You need never worry about the future of such a horse if for any reason you may have to part with him. You assure him of friends wherever he goes. Perhaps the greatest kindness you can do any horse is to educate him well."

Thomas Alexander Roberts was born on September 15th 1900 in Bangalore, India, to Rosina and John Roberts. Records indicate that John, reportedly of wealthy Welsh ancestry, was father to eleven children. John Roberts was stationed in India while serving in the British Army and rose to the rank of Warrant Officer, but was later invalided back to England where he died of a heart attack in 1909. He had become a Rough Rider during Army service, as did five of his six sons, including Tom.

Rosina gave birth to Tom's youngest sister, Ivy, shortly after his father died. The family was left with a small pension, and an allowance for each child under fourteen years of five pounds per annum. Aged around eleven, Tom was admitted to the Duke of York Military Academy in Dover. This was a residential school for the orphaned sons of soldiers.

When the First World War broke out, Tom followed in his father's footsteps and joined the British Army as a boy trumpeter. It was a week after his fourteenth birthday. The prevalence of trench warfare meant that trumpeters and drummers were phased out – so many boys had been killed that public outcry led to their being withdrawn from battle areas.

So, Tom didn't leave England, but as part of the Royal Field Artillery was sent to Woolwich for his training, where he was taught to ride.

"I soon noticed that by good luck, or something, I seemed to have 'a knack' with horses… The trumpeter needed to be a fair horseman at least, have a well-schooled horse he could manage, and all horses had to be taught to lead well under difficulties."

Here we can see the kernel of the horseman Tom was to become. At Woolwich he was under the command of men who brought with

Tom and his first wife, Ruby.

them a tradition of training cavalry horses and were capable instructors. Tom was exposed to a vast array of horses, many of which came with problem behaviours. Army hierarchy meant the best behaved horses went to officers.

Although Tom doesn't document where he learned the value of the "Go-forward" lesson it was a mandatory requirement for any horse in battle to move forward unconditionally, both on the ground and under saddle – lives, and victory, depended on it. His skills were born out of a time when horses had a job to do and were obliged to perform.

The British Cavalry worked with the French School of Equitation in Saumur and, here, the French manual outlines the requirements of a Cavalry officer and his horse.

The superior school of horsemanship is merely the normal development and the exact application of the principles which serve as the basis of all horsemanship. It teaches the officer to preserve even in the midst of the greatest difficulties, a perfect and firm seat, with justice and fineness in the application of his aids, combined with an absolute discretion in their employment.

It teaches, in fact, the ease and correctness of position, which proves the control of the rider over himself and the clear free working of his mind. It searches for constant forward impulsion in the horse, calm absolute obedience, and a position rigorously straight and balanced, in the execution of all movements.

Lieut. Col. Blacque Belair
Chief Instructor at the Cavalry School, Saumur, France
Cavalry Horsemanship and Horse Training 1919

And in the foreword to this manual, Major Malcolm Borwick, of the Royal Scots Greys and a Commandant with the Cavalry Corp Equitation School, writes of the importance of sound training of the horses required for duties during the war:

It has, I think, been conclusively proved, more than ever during the present war, that any time spent on Equitation, whether applied to trooper or troop horse, has not been wasted. As the life-taking mechanical appliances improve in efficiency, so must the Cavalry, by means of their training, increase their power to manoeuvre rapidly, and adopt with the maximum speed and smoothness, formations which are at the same time elastic and comprehensive... Equitation is the basis on which the whole training of Cavalry rests; the sound principles, the logical sequence, and, above all, the clear explanation, all go to make this book the greatest help towards the attainment of this end.

Britain's Cavalry mounts were initially sourced from the country's supply of horses and they were assigned to one of the three artillery groups. Each of these groups had a specific role dictated by the style and weight of ammunition in use. While most horses sourced for the war effort were already working horses and tractable, those that were deemed 'difficult' or in need of further training were referred to the battery's 'rough rider'. This position was highly valued and the rider's duties were rewarded with an extra six pence a day of pay.

A year or so into the war the Army knew it was facing a critical shortage of rough riders and the decision was made to run an emergency three-month course. During peace-time this would have been allotted nine months. Tom's skill with horses had clearly been recognised and his commanding officers recommended his inclusion. Whether deliberate or not, the memo calling for nominations didn't state the usual minimum age of eighteen.

The course was tough and attrition took its toll. Tom lost about thirteen kilograms of weight in the first month! But he clearly had the required fortitude and early in 1917, while still only sixteen, Trumpeter Tom Roberts became the British Army's youngest ever rough rider.

While his Unit was stationed at Boyton, Tom was responsible for the training of 25 horses and mules a week as remounts for the front lines in

France. On page 62 of his first book 'Horse Control and the Bit', published in 1971, Tom recounts the value of what he calls 'The Go-forward lesson' to 'a pair of mules that had wrecked the front of a wagon by kicking at the use of the whip'. It's mentioned in the context of helping the reader to understand the importance of breaking lessons down into small parts, something modern horse trainers call shaping.

Tom's room at Boyton. "I am holding a photo of my mother. The cards and photos on the wall, I placed there around my bed." This photo was taken at Boyton, near Codford, Salisbury Plain, England, 1916 or early 1917.

Tom is also talking about the need to have a clear, exclusive signal for every response.

"The first essential to obedience is understanding, and this requires the establishment of a language of some sort or other that can be understood by both man and a horse: a simple basic language. We try to get him to understand certain things mean 'start' or 'go faster', others mean, 'stop' or 'go slower' and still others, 'change direction'. Simple as they are, these basic things have to be taught. The better you can teach, the less trouble you will have later."

This is probably a good place to let you know that in the second half of this book you can expect more detailed analysis of how Tom Roberts' work comes together in a practical fashion and why it is so highly regarded by the modern trainers who train in accordance with the horse's unique capacities to learn.

Equitation Science would have appealed to Tom as he had a scientist's mind – always curious, open to new information, prepared to challenge conventional wisdom when necessary and a drive to know how things worked. He was not afraid to experiment and welcomed collaboration. One of his students remarked about Tom:

"He was always exploring his own theories, and he invited Bill Reed and myself while Thorpe McConville and Webb McKelvey were out, both American top horsemen... every Wednesday night we would meet and talk about the differences in horsemanship in Western Trail Riding, Australian Stock Horses, Camp Drafting, and what it came back to was, basically, you train every horse when you break them in."

Bernie Biggs – Former Stockman and Eventer,
student of Tom Roberts.

RIDING ESTABLISHMENT.

ROYAL HORSE ARTILLERY.

Equitation Certificate.

Rank _____ Name _____

Duration of Course : From _____ to _____

HORSEMANSHIP.

CAPABILITIES AS A TRAINER OF REMOUNTS.

HORSEMASTERSHIP.

CAPABILITIES AS A REGIMENTAL INSTRUCTOR.

REMARKS.

Chief Instructor.

COLONEL, R.H.A.
COMMANDING RIDING ESTABLISHMENT, R.H.A.
Superintendent.

Kirkee, India, 1st October 1922, taken by Mrs Rhodes.

Chapter Two

Profit You, Profit You Not

"Tom was the first person to say 'Profit you, profit you not'. I think that in all his early training in England, and when he was in The Army, he had worked out this method of communicating with horses. Say a horse won't go forward, and he keeps pressing it to make it go forward: the moment it went forward he would relax and make a fuss of the horse so that it knows that it's done the right thing. He was very gentle, and very slow, and he would just keep trying to get the horse to understand what he wanted, and as soon as the horse did understand what he wanted, then he would relax and make a fuss of it, and all the rest of it, or finish for the day."

Elisabeth Garran – lifelong friend of Tom and his wife, Pat.

In his teachings, Tom often referred to the lessons he learned in the British Army. These were clearly formative years and what an education to have – accelerated and intensified by the need to produce safe, reliable remounts combined with the benefits of working within a knowledgeable institution. Plus, simply the sheer numbers of horses helped consolidate his learning.

Along with Tom's natural aptitude and interest this environment fostered not only his riding skills but also his knowledge of horse care and psychology. In later chapters we'll explore this in more detail.

The war years naturally took a toll on the Army's cavalry and equestrian training – so many men and horses had been lost. Incredibly though, as the Army demobilised there were an estimated one million horses and mules that were to be 'disposed of'. Saved from the fate of being shipped to the continent for slaughter and human consumption, around 500 of these equine war veterans were destined to join Tom in the next phase of his equestrian education.

Shortly after the end of the war, a parcel of land in the parish of Weedon Bec, Northamptonshire, had been secured as the site from which the Army would restore its Artillery riding. The Army School of Equitation was led by Major Charles 'Taffy' Walwyn, who when sourcing horses for his students included those that had a reputation for being difficult. This course was going to be no easy ride!

As soon as Tom heard of the Instructor's Course with Major Walwyn he let his commanding officers know he was keen to attend. They recommended his enrolment and in July 1919, Tom joined the ranks at Weedon to begin the nine-month course. By this time, he was probably suffering no illusions as to how tough the training might be, but again the military machinations ensured only the most resilient men made it through.

"By the end of the first week of this, the first class, about half the men accepted for the course had been returned to their units as unacceptable, "Not up to the required standard". By the end of the second week most of those remaining had asked to be returned to their units. Permission was refused."

This illustration on page 16 of Reminiscences looks to be the cover of a handwritten record of Tom's training on the Instructors' course. How we would have loved to read this while researching this book, but it hasn't yet come to light.

Major Walywn went on to become one of Britain's leading showjumpers and he made sure that jumping was a critical focus at Weedon. Horses and riders had to be capable of jumping anything, under any conditions. There is film preserved from exercises in the fixed jumping lanes and fields around the Equitation School. The precision and scope of the drills are like nothing seen today. While the film shows the finished, polished product, Tom's description of how jump training was approached at Weedon demonstrates an appreciation of the need to shape the training of the individual horse in order to build technique and confidence.

The nine months Tom spent at Weedon certainly became a platform for his life with horses. By the way, Tom never actually owned a performance horse. His efforts were always dedicated to starting or improving horses which belonged to others. This is remarkable as many modern horse trainers are inclined to stake their reputation on a horse or two that they produce. Tom had so many horses on which to hone his skills that he never needed this kind of publicity.

Towards the end of the course the students had a guest instructor. Capt. J. J. (Jimmy) Pearce had been engaged to lecture and demonstrate his training methods. He came with his own team of horses and what he had to share made a lasting impact on Tom.

Captain Pearce must have arrived at Weedon with quite a reputation. American born, he'd trained horses for a variety of sporting pursuits and been a successful exhibitor in Championships at New York's Madison Square Gardens. Some of the details are difficult to verify, but we have no reason not to believe Tom's account. Capt. Pearce had also performed in the famous Buffalo Bill shows but after receiving an inheritance had decided to pursue classical dressage in Europe. While his original plan was to train with Frenchman James Fillis, this didn't come to fruition (Fillis had taken up service with the Czar of Russia), and as a fall-back he applied to join the Spanish Riding School in Vienna for which he was accepted. Captain Pearce spent several years there under the tutelage of Johann Meixner and was himself in great demand. Tom describes Pearce as 'a very accomplished horseman: a very great horseman.'

In Chapter Six of 'Reminiscences' Tom details the visit of Captain Pearce and how deeply it affected him.

"A few days watching this expert completely deflated me. He brought me to understand that although I had good natural ability I still had to learn how to apply it. That in itself was a valuable lesson for me. I still had to learn how to apply any ability I might have – Capt. James Pearce set me searching for more."

It was during Pearce's visit that Tom gained an insight into the value of taking time to solve a problem, and the need to have a clear process in mind before tackling a challenging behaviour. He emphasises the importance of PREPARATION in the closing pages of 'Reminiscences' as one of his greatest life lessons.

Another tip Tom took from Captain Pearce has been passed on to further generations of riders and it's one that Australian Olympian, Erica Taylor, still uses routinely.

"The one thing I always remember from Robbie, and I still teach it to this day, and I tear my hair that people don't, was to teach the horse to stretch the rein. He'd learnt that from Captain J. J. Pearce… He used to imitate his voice, and say 'Teach him to streeeeeeeeetch the rein'… It was the first thing with a young horse he used to advocate, and I've done it all my life. Teach the horse to stretch the rein: in other words, teach the horse to take the rein. I see so often now, that people do not teach them to take the rein. I can't remember his exact words, but we just did it. You let the horse take the rein so that he stretches down and still sat on the bit. If you want a horse to lengthen his stride, he has to lengthen his frame and to do that he has to reach for the bit. It's so simple really."

Erica Taylor – Olympic Dressage rider and student of Tom

Captain Pearce also coached the Oxford University Polo Club and later published two books, 'The Horse Rampant' and 'Everybody's Polo'. A third, 'A Lifetime with Horses' was never published but was printed in serial form by the *Hoofs & Horns* magazine. Tom maintained contact with Captain Pearce and helped to facilitate his visits to Australia in the 1950s where he assisted in the preparation of the Australian Olympic team.

Tom passed the final examination at Weedon very capably, and he was always proud of the comments recorded on his certificate.

A first class man in every way. Intelligent, keen and smart with plenty of pluck and energy. A very good horseman. Will make a good instructor.

In the breakdown of the final examination Tom came second on the day and lost only one of the military riding tasks – the 'Sabre vs Sabre'. He was dux of the Equitation Course. Good going for a man whose formal education finished at 14 years of age.

To India

When his instructor training was finished Tom was given the offer to stay at Weedon as Assistant Instructor, but he had other plans. While he had no memories of his place of birth, India held a fascination and he took a posting as Rough Rider with the 95th Battery, Royal Field Artillery. He was stationed at Kirkee, near Poona in the Bombay region.

Again, Tom's choices and the opportunity they presented contributed enormously to the horseman he became; the man who went on to himself influence the lives of so many people and horses.

Tom devotes a good few chapters of his final book detailing his experiences in India – from polo ponies – to biters that bolted – to carriage horses – confirmed jibbers – racehorses that wouldn't win and children's ponies that refused to get up.

One story Tom was particularly fond of re-telling was his experience with a horse that wouldn't cross water. In the style of J. J. Pearce he sat patiently for hours until the horse changed his mind. Tom said it was one of the few times he wished he was a smoker!

This and all his other encounters served to give Tom more tools for his workbox but above all, he kept returning to the lesson that stayed with him for life... 'Go forward, dear'.

Part of the class instructed by Sergeant T.A. Roberts to qualify as riding instructors at Kirkee, India, 1921.

Tom in India, date unknown.

Tom at the South Australian Police Barracks. Photo SA Police Historical Society.

Chapter Three

Down Under

Tom Roberts never returned to England. At the end of his army service Tom, like all who had served their time, was entitled to the compensation of settlement in one of Britain's colonies. Soldiers could elect to return home or become 'soldier settlers' elsewhere in the British Empire. Tom chose Australia, and sailed into Port Adelaide on January 4th 1924 to start a new life Down Under. With him were his wife, Ruby, and their infant daughter, Mabel, who had been born while they were stationed in India. Tom and Ruby's second child, Denis, was born in 1926.

Determined to take any work to support his family, Tom set out to join his brother Bert, and his wife, Molly, at Wolseley near Bordertown in South Australia. Here he took on a variety of labouring jobs, relishing the hard work and coping well with the Australian heat. It wasn't long though, before his skills drew him to horse work and in characteristic fashion, Tom's keen powers of observation were at work – although perhaps not in the following story!

By his own admission the circumstances that led to another insight into horse behaviour occurred due to Tom's own miscalculation. He had taken work as an apiarist, or bee-keeper. The Tatiara district from where he worked is big gum country and the pickings for bees then would have made this occupation far more viable than it is today. Tom had learned the tricks of the trade and thought it a better option than the vagaries of regular farming. In order to set out on his own he bought a horse, Nugget, and a cart.

Nugget was not enamoured with the notion of going forward and his propensity to stand stock still was a virtue for an apiarist while he gathered hives and bees. Tom had been told of a natural hive on the branch of a native she-oak tree which he set about capturing early one morning. The branch was too high to reach easily so he thought it would be a good idea to position the cart beneath the hive, the better to drop it down into Tom's waiting, empty hive. Simple...

Well, all was going well until Tom accidentally knocked the hive with his head, sending it crashing onto the back and hindquarters of the snoozing Nugget. Within the chaos caused by the angry bees and Nugget's efforts to flee Tom made a critical observation about how horses react to pain.

In short, when Nugget's running didn't succeed in removing the stinging bees his next coping choice was to kick and strike incessantly. Tom observes:

"One thing this lively incident clearly demonstrates is the fact that if a horse finds going forward does not cause a discontinuation or reduction of any pain he is being subjected to, be it whip or anything else like the bees, he will try something different."

Here is the critical essence of how and why horse training relies on the handler's ability to motivate a horse with pressure, and release it as soon as the horse offers the desired response. When pressure is unrelenting or the trainer gets the timing of the release wrong, the horse can quickly trial another, perhaps unwelcome, coping mechanism.

Tom goes on to observe how Nugget, from that day on, was ruined as an apiarist's cart horse for the slightest buzzing would send him into a frenzy – the behaviour he had learned was his best defence. He'd done what all horses do so superbly in their natural environment, associated a previously innocuous noise with a threat to his survival. Tom warns his readers that horses should never be housed near hives because if they upset one, the hapless horse is at real risk of being stung to death.

I want this man

The post war economic downturn was starting to have an impact in Australia and Tom was looking to a more secure future. He had a Government job in mind and he initially applied to join the Australian Army but it had ceased recruiting. So had the Police Force, but it made an exception for Tom.

"The (Army) Recruiting Officer then gave me a letter of introduction to Police Inspector W. Johns, who was in charge of the South Australian Mounted Police. Bill Johns told me that they, too, had been ordered not to take on any more men. He then looked at my military papers, asked quite a number of questions – and rang the Commissioner of Police. I heard him say: 'I want this man, Sir'."

With those words began Tom's new career with the South Australian Police Force, giving him job security through the Depression years and again leading him to a professional involvement with horses. As a policeman, Tom's employment contract excluded him from receiving any money for services outside the department, but this didn't stop him from taking on mostly difficult horses for re-education and travelling as far as practicable in his off duty hours to help owners. He joined the

Thebarton barracks in 1948, home of the South Australian Mounted Police with Sergeant Tom Roberts (holding the tail) and 'the boys'.

Adelaide Polo Club, where his experience playing in India meant he was in demand to help set ponies 'on the right track'.

This, and the 'policeman's lot' was Tom's life for more than a decade and he was, by all accounts, capable, showed a strong sense of duty and was not without the ability to see human nature with a healthy dose of good humour. His progress through the ranks, though, was stymied by an incident in the police barracks in 1933 which resulted in Tom being demoted. He fought hard against what he saw as an unjust ruling – this was eventually overturned but he never received compensatory back pay.

According to records, Tom had loaned his police motorbike to another officer. When it wasn't returned in a state of cleanliness to his standard, he took his colleague to task. Blows followed and both men were initially found culpable.

Tom and Ruby divorced in the early 1930s and this must have been a trying time because not only was it The Great Depression, but he was now sole parent to his two young children and had a demanding job. Tom swore never to marry again.

A year into World War II, Hitler's threatening advances motivated Tom to again join the armed forces. He took leave from the police force to serve with the Australian Army and this time, he was at the upper age limit for recruits. In 1940, aged 39 and only a few weeks short of the age cut-off, Tom began duties with the 2/7th Field Regiment, which was despatched to North Africa. The regiment fought at El Alamein in 1942, at what was the first land victory for Allied forces, and stopping the enemy here arguably lessened the threat to Australia.

Although it was forbidden, Tom kept a diary throughout his service. He also managed to take and retain photos during his overseas postings.

Thankfully, Tom's war diaries were preserved and eight booklets of closely written script were returned to him after his discharge from the Army in 1947. They were published posthumously and present a valuable first-hand account of the time, as well as giving the reader an insight into Tom's compassion and appreciation for humanity. "Will we be disappointed after?" met with very favourable reviews. This, from Tony Baker writing for *The Advertiser:*

He (Tom) kept a diary and at one point wrote: "Frightened? I was frightened beyond all description. It's the uncertainty and the inability to do anything about it that gets to you" ... This, in the unvarnished people's language of the day is how it felt, looked and smelt for an ordinary man to leave Adelaide and fight in a distant country... on leave in 1943, Tom Roberts wrote "I have passed this way innumerable times before but it is not until now with the poverty and distress of the Middle East fresh in mind that I am conscious of the beauty and contentment and prosperity of our homes and people." Simple enough words but they ring like bells.

Tom's diaries are a gift of insight into the experiences of the generations who served their country with pride.

When Tom returned to South Australia and police duties, he found his services had been requested by the Mounted Division to take up the role as Sergeant Instructor. This division and its horses had been in recess during the war years; the head of the Mounted Division, Inspector W.H. King, knew that Tom was the man for the job. There was much to be done – horses to be bought and trained, new recruits to train, as well as the daily duties of the Police Greys.

Tom was in his element and along with an enthusiastic team of riders, set about invigorating the Thebarton barracks as well as the Greys' presence in open competitions. One particular horse, Quarter, who had been found on the rodeo circuit, was to become a real crowd favourite.

1955 Melbourne Show with Tom judging the Police Horse events.

The SA Mounted Police regularly competed in competitions, seen here in full flight over hurdles.

One of the advances Tom advocated, which may be traced back to his jumping instruction under Taffy Walwyn at Weedon, was to make sure the police horses were trained to jump. In those days the horses saw more active service; duties that would now be performed by specialised vehicles. When one of Adelaide's iconic stores, Moore's, went up in flames the police horses were in attendance. One of them refused to cross a fire fighters' water hose, and Tom used this event to push for jump training to be mandatory for all police horses.

He succeeded in persuading the then Commissioner, and very soon the Police Greys and their riders became strong competitors in events throughout South Australia. Police Horse Quarter was assigned to MC Frank Patterson and they went on to win many jumping trophies and horse trials.

To give you a sense of just how active the horse community was in the post war decade, in the December of 1955 alone, there were forty shows or gymkhanas in or around Adelaide. Every local oval held a gymkhana once a year. Horses were kept in backyards. Erica Taylor paints a picture for us:

"I moved down from the country, up near Melrose, and, much against my parents' wishes, I managed to find a place to keep two horses that I had... I found a little paddock behind what is now The Northern Hotel, on Regency Road near the Main North Road intersection. It was a little almond orchard behind there that was about a quarter of an acre, I suppose, behind where Woolworths and all those big stores are now... I used to ride my horse through the back streets to Hackney Rd, then through Victoria Park racecourse and on down to the Greenhill Road grounds, once a fortnight, and have lessons. Sometimes I took both horses."

Erica Taylor – Olympian

People routinely rode from their homes to events, and the parklands that surround Adelaide city housed many horses.

"The Council were fairly generous with their land at that stage: there were still signs up saying 'Cows Only', or 'Horses' on The Park Lands. The Lord Mayor lived in Walkerville and had a team of polo ponies in his backyard: this was tolerated back then."

Rob Goldsworthy – Dressage Trainer and Competitor

Elisabeth Garran, who we heard from earlier, was one of the young riders who frequented the Park Lands. This is where she met Tom Roberts, mounted on one of the most difficult horses he'd come across, Elkedra.

"He used to ride Elkedra 'round the Park Lands. I used to ride my horse that I got in 1947. I always used to talk to anyone with a lovely horse, which Elkedra was. I'd go riding before school and after school around The North Park Lands. Robbie was very friendly, and we used to talk a lot. I was very interested in the European way of riding: it changed the way you sat, it changed the way you controlled the horse, the way the horse moved, everything. Robbie was very interested in this as well, so we used to have these long discussions. In those days

Erica Taylor and Crown Law on a visit from Tom in The Dauntless Dowager.

there were a lot of riding clubs. People would just go riding on a Saturday in a group; a social thing, just for a nice ride, then, at the end, they'd go to someone's house and have lots of lovely food. They all behaved very nicely. Most weren't interested in achieving the things we were hearing about from the people who came from Europe, but some of them were. Robbie gave them demonstrations sometimes."

Elisabeth Garran

Elkedra, named after Elkedra station, had been a successful racehorse in the Northern Territory but when the war years interrupted racing, his owner sent him south as a gift to Miss Dorothy Mansom, a successful rider and amateur opera singer.

Elkedra was a handful, even for an experienced rider like Miss Mansom, and the story of how Tom came to form a partnership with this animal is inextricably linked to meeting the love of his life.

Tom and Pat Roberts on their wedding day.

Chapter Four

Never Say Never

"I think Tom was a remarkable gentleman. For sure, I don't remember the colour of his eyes, but I know the girls will."

Rob Goldsworthy

They were blue by the way – 'vivid blue', according to one former student. As a confirmed bachelor in uniform and a gentleman who had a way with horses, Tom Roberts must have fluttered a few of the ladies' hearts.

In 1947, Dorothy Mansom had asked Tom to take on her nine-year-old brown thoroughbred, Elkedra, with the goal of educating him as a hack. Having raced most of his life and even won the Alice Springs Cup, Elkedra came with some baggage which made him a difficult, if not dangerous, ride. He was especially frightened of cows and horse drawn vehicles. Tom used to ride him through the Adelaide Park Lands on most days.

"There were still many bakers and milk-carts drawn by horses: every time Elkedra saw a horse drawn vehicle, or a cow, no matter how far away it might be, he would really start to throw himself about. Never an easy horse to ride, I found him very difficult during these incidents... He was now being well-fed

Elkedra, named after Elkedra Station, came to Tom with his fair share of issues.

and expertly cared for, and was beginning to feel like a time-bomb when ridden. However, he had the making of a first class hack."

Dressage was just starting to get a following in Australia at this time, and Tom's exposure to it through his Army days gave him a key to guiding Elkedra through his re-education and fear. Tom discovered that the horse wasn't fond of going sideways – this makes sense as he was bred and trained to run. However, in teaching Elkedra to yield sideways on cue Tom managed to diminish his aversion to the cows and horse drawn vehicles. Any time Elkedra started to get tense he was asked for a 'half-pass' and this proved a real turning point. He went on to perform successfully with Miss Mansom and 'be just the horse she had hoped he would become'. Tom also later used him for demonstrations and Elkedra was ridden by J. J. Pearce when he visited South Australia in 1951.

Patricia Rose

Elkedra's influence on Tom's life, though, went further than raising his profile as a trainer. Dorothy Mansom had worked in the Rationing Commission during World War II, and it was there that she formed a friendship with a Miss Patricia Rose. They had discovered their mutual interest in horses and routinely rode out together on weekends with Pat on board Elkedra. When it was decided that the horse needed expert re-training Sergeant Tom Roberts was invited to take on the task.

"Talking and riding Elkedra that first afternoon had taken several hours, then we had a meal, followed by more talk with some of Dorothy's friends... the time flew past – and it was not until 11.30 that Miss Patricia Rose realised that even if she left immediately, she would be lucky to catch the last tram."

Tom gave Pat a lift back to her boarding home on his motorbike, where they were met by a disapproving Miss Potter, who ran the home for country girls. Pat was 23 years younger than Tom, and while Tom acknowledged the wisdom in Miss Potter's reservations, it held no sway when it came to the matter of love. Tom, the self-avowed bachelor, was smitten.

Patricia Rose grew up surrounded by horses on 'Corrumbene', the farm of her pioneering family in South Australia's Hindmarsh Valley. Her favourite mount was Kirrup, which Pat used to deliver refreshments to the men working in the fields. When the polio outbreak of the late 1930s forced the closure of many schools Pat was determined to further her education, and rode her trusty horse to Victor Harbor High School where she learned to type and take shorthand; this led to her 'war job' with the Rationing Commission.

Horses, however, were not Pat's only passion.

"In memory of a close cousin in the RAAF, Henry George Rose, who had been killed over Belgium I entered a Flying Scholarship at Parafield, and in 1949 obtained my private flying licence... I felt it was an extension of riding... my first longer trip was to take my 'next-door riding friend of earlier days', for a flight over our homes at Victor Harbor. I don't think we told our parents until afterwards!!!"

Pat Roberts

Pat was a founding member of the Australian Women Pilots' Association and took on this task as she did everything in life, with competency and good cheer.

Tom and Pat married in 1952. Their wedding was put off for a week as it clashed with the first One Day Event in South Australia where Tom ran the dressage phase and Pat pencilled for one of the judges, Captain J.J. Pearce.

Together, they contributed enormously to the education of South Australia's riders and horses. Pat took up film making as a hobby and soon became a fixture with her trusty 8mm camera anywhere Tom visited to teach and train. Their home on West Beach Road, at Richmond, became a hub for visiting trainers, and students were offered instruction evenings. Tom would talk on the latest topic he'd been investigating, Pat's films were viewed and discussed, and then tea and cake was served as the evenings wound up. One film evening they organised drew 200 guests!

"The instruction evenings at the house were just so much fun. Everybody would come, and it would be a real social night, and Pat would put on her movies which she'd taken, because she used to film just about all the lessons, a lot of the competitions, and she used to make sure that she got everybody. She didn't just focus on whoever might have been winning. She got everybody. So you would come to these nights, and you would be sure that you would see yourself. Of course, at that stage, you didn't have videos and whatever: just the old movies. So you would see yourself on the movie, on the screen they used to put up. It was so good."

Pat Hutchens – former student and current dressage judge

"I can't remember what night of the week they were held on, but I know that you never wanted to miss them. These were the classes at Pat and Robbie's house. We'd go along and listen to Robbie instruct on various things and watch the ciné movies that Pat had taken of the latest – either competition, or horse loading thing. Whatever was happening: she was there with her ciné camera.

We all loved going there. We'd talk for hours and hours, and Pat would come in at about a quarter past nine, and say 'Tea?' Every time we went to her house, ever, even when I went recently: 'Tea?' She was just gorgeous, and, of course, you'd have to try to get Robbie to stop talking, and we all wanted to listen. So, we'd all have a cup of tea or coffee or something or other, and a bit of supper, and then we'd still want to keep talking. She'd virtually have to kick us out of the house. They were a very generous couple, just fascinating to be around: they were just amazing."

Rita Baker, nee Quorn-Smith – former student and later assistant to Tom

Pat and Tom's union was an enduring and tender partnership that influenced so many areas of equestrian life throughout Australia and beyond. Pat was a consummate record keeper and organiser. Her 'hobby' of film making evolved into a large library that documented life events and Tom's work with horses; an outstanding legacy that warrants preservation.

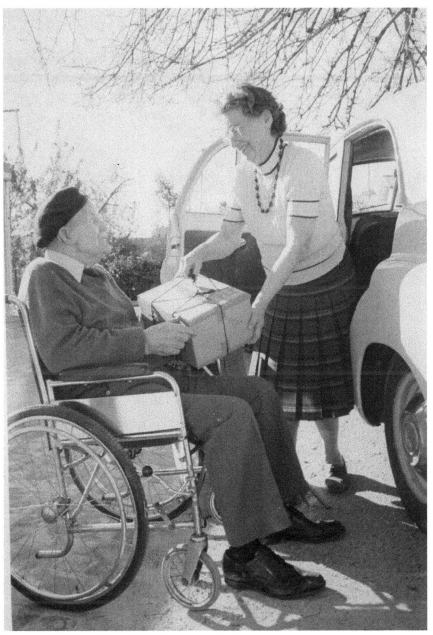

Tom and Pat Roberts.

Tom was in a class of his own as an instructor.

Chapter Five

Weedon's Way

"I think the books really are Tom's legacy, and what he did in Hoofs & Horns, that was very good too. What he wrote in there once a month was fantastic. People knew that he was 'Weedon'. I think he started off by doing it quietly and everyone found out who it was anyway. He gave lots of horse keeping tips to people who had no-one to help them."

Rob Goldsworthy, Past President of Equestrian Australia,
South Australian Branch, dressage rider and trainer

The next three decades of Robbie's life were incredibly productive and marked by many 'firsts'.

Mounted on Elkedra, Tom won the first Dressage Event held by an agricultural show, at the 1950 Adelaide Royal Show. He wasn't fond of competitive riding but encouraged his students to take part as a test of their training, and always avoided riding against his own pupils.

"The Riding Club next door used to run a dressage competition. It might have been just at the end of the year, or something. I remember, I went down for a lesson with Robbie, and then I went over, because it was on the same grounds on Greenhill Road, and I went in this Dressage test: the first test I ever

rode. And I won it. And I came back and said to Robbie 'Oh, wow! Robbie! I won!' and he said 'Oh, yes. Thought you would'. I was flabbergasted."

Erica Taylor, South Australia's first dressage Olympian,

describing her first dressage success on Beau Ray

The Dressage Club of South Australia (DCSA) had been formed in 1950, the first of its kind in Australia and a club that is still active, running regular dressage competitions in the Adelaide Hills. Pat was its patron and a familiar face at competitions until her death in 2014.

The DCSA was started by Tom and Dorothy Mansom, with Pat as Assistant Secretary. One of the catalysts to its formation was to host Captain Pearce on a visit to Australia, at the invitation of R.M. Williams who was keen to foster the development of dressage. Australian horsemanship at that time was regarded (not least by Australians) as the best in the world and to many this new, fancy stuff called 'dressage' was seen as unnecessary and elitist.

Interest grew, though, and the club had an enthusiastic founding membership which worked to educate any who were interested in this 'new' style of horsemanship by seeking the input of European dressage trainers.

"This club helped the great majority of Continental horsemen coming to S.A., one of whom was a young Polish born rider, Marian Malecki, … and another great, Franz Mairinger, became Australia's first national dressage coach. His pupils won our first Olympic Equestrian Bronze and Gold Medals. The Club had been formed to welcome to Australia Capt. J.J. Pearce, then in his eighties, who had been a pupil of one of the very great instructors at the Spanish Riding School in Vienna – and at Saumur in France."

Pat Roberts

Tom was Chief Instructor and classes were held every Sunday in the South Adelaide Park Lands, east of the current bowling club on South Terrace. Other classes were also formed around Adelaide, with Tom as guest instructor.

"Back when we had large classes, before individual instruction became popular, we did a little drill riding, and that was a good breakaway from the strict regime we had developed because time was so important. We had so little time: just a few hours a couple of days at the weekend, or maybe only one, and so much ground to cover. I remember that Tom said that 'What we find is that the instruction taken over this year comes to fruition the following year'. It takes a little while for the pennies to drop. One had to be fairly patient, and being a rider yourself, you had to relate to what the riders were experiencing. Tom really did set the precedent for riding instruction, because he would get on the horse and demonstrate. I think that is the only way of really knowing the rider's problems."

Keith Guster – DCSA Instructor

Tom had a real gift for imparting knowledge to his students and set a precedent for riding instruction.

Keith Guster was mentored by Tom through an instructor training course he instigated for club members. It was based on his curriculum and notes from Weedon and took four years to complete. Other instructor graduates who went on to be influential trainers included Pat Hutchens and Sandra O'Brien.

Keith recalls being awed by Tom's mastery with a horse that attended at the club training one day and reared its way through the entire lesson. At the end the frustrated rider handed the reins to Tom – it continued to rear but was set 'on the right track' when Tom stood up in his stirrups as the horse was almost vertical and firmly rattled the bit on one side. The horse soon learned that rearing would 'profit you not'.

"I was blessed to have been associated with Tom. He was way ahead of his time. He was such a knowledgeable man, and such a fair man. I can remember him saying to me 'Look Keith, not only must you be fair, but you must be seen to be fair'. That, I thought, I must endeavour to carry out."

Keith Guster

Rita Baker, who worked closely with Tom in his later years especially, couldn't recall a horse with which he didn't succeed.

"I could see sometimes that he didn't know what to do: different horses, especially ones off the track, had had different things done with them. Someone at the instruction classes might ask a question and he'd say, 'I'll let you know next week'. He didn't actually say, 'I'll work on this and think about it and we'll work out what the problem is and how to fix it', but that was the concept. The next week he would come back with an idea of what we might do to fix the problem. Sometimes it was the rider. Sometimes it was the horse. It was getting the horse's confidence in you and knowing what you required of it. It wasn't just making the horse do what you want, it was getting the horse to understand, because he said that most of the time they want to do what you want, it's just getting them to understand what you want and then getting them to be able to

do it. I think Robbie was so good, because he was learning at the same time. He was always learning himself."

In the process of learning Tom made some lasting friendships. One was with the American ranchman, Webb McKelvey. The two were introduced by Webb's son, Mike, who had taken an interest in articles written by Tom in the iconic magazine of the day, *Hoofs & Horns*. Tom wrote for the magazine, founded by R.M. Williams, on a wide range of topics related to the horse, its psychology, care and training. He reported on events under the pen-name 'Weedon'.

Webb McKelvey can be seen in Tom's ground-breaking second book 'Horse Control – The Young Horse' demonstrating his methods for starting young horses. Tom clearly saw much to admire in his calm, common-sense and horse friendly approach. In later years, when on a visit to Australia, Webb asked his son to take him to see Tom at his home. He required a stop at a sweet shop first and then asked Mike to park the car outside the house. Sitting in the car, Webb produced from the bag of sweets a toy that came with chocolate 'Bertie Beetles' – it made a distinctive click when pressed on its back. Webb sat, clicking away, until Tom, curious, shuffled out to investigate the source. Webb revealed his trick much to the amusement of all, and handed the Bertie Beetle to Tom before he left. The Bertie Beetle was put to creative use by Tom with his students. He carried it in his pocket and when he felt his pupils were losing their focus, he'd reach for the beetle and start clicking. Before long, their attention was regained and the lesson continued. This was long before the popularised 'clicker training' of dogs and horses, which is used in a different fashion to Tom's! Readers familiar with Learning Theory will recognise that Tom's use was in the quadrant of negative reinforcement.

Tom was always fair with his contemporaries and was not inclined to let ego cloud his judgement. In 1972, the editor of *Hoofs & Horns* sought

Tom's opinion on a matter of professional jealousy. J.D Wilton and his troupe of 'Wonder Horses and White Alsatian Wonder Dogs' who signed his letters 'Australia's Greatest Master Horseman' had issued a challenge to a horse breaking contest and he was keen to showcase his methods against those of Kell Jeffery (aged in his nineties at the time) or advocate and author of The Jeffery Method, Mr Maurice Wright.

Wilton wrote, *'I could give him (Maurice Wright) the lesson of his life on the scientific catching, mouthing, handling, leading and general education of the unbroken horse, and thoroughly convince him of the stupidity of what he is writing about the Jeffery Method.'*

By contrast, Tom's response is filled with humanity, observing that, *'the trouble with many good horsemen is that they can never see any virtue in any other horseman… all these methods are good and all remarkably similar when you get down to brass tacks… but lots of the great horsemen do not KNOW what they do – or do not ALWAYS know. It's a gift they have and they just have it. It's a completely different thing to teaching it.'*

He closes his letter saying, *'I like Jeffery though. We would get on. I admired Wilton's results but I don't know how he gets them not having seen his books… One thing about writing is you have to think hard before you put it down. It makes you sort out your ideas.'*

Among other equestrian firsts for which Tom worked was the formation of the Equestrian Federation of Australia, now known as Equestrian Australia, to ensure that Australia was represented at the 1956 Olympics. Tom, like many others of the day, was keen to see our country and horses compete on the world stage, and for that they needed a national body. This was ratified just in time for an Australian team to travel to Stockholm in 1956, as quarantine laws made it untenable for horses from the northern hemisphere to compete in Melbourne. The Australian team finished fourth at its first Olympics and, in 1960 at Rome, won gold under the tutelage of Franz Mairinger.

It could be argued that if not for Tom, Franz Mairinger's talents may not have been available to Australian equestrians. Franz was Austrian born and had been educated in High School dressage at the Spanish Riding School in Vienna. His family had suffered great losses during the course of World War II and he emigrated to Australia in 1952, sponsored by R.M. Williams. By the time he arrived, his contracted position as a horse trainer, as well as his accommodation, had been filled so he took work initially as a labourer and upholsterer while deciding whether it was viable to bring his family to Australia.

One day, while working on the docks at Port Adelaide, Franz cut his hand and needed medical attention. In the process of sewing him up the doctor learned of Franz's former life and skill with a horse. He also knew Tom and suggested the two meet.

It must have been a most exciting meeting for these two dedicated horsemen. Tom says he learned a great deal from Franz and he always wrote with the thought of Franz reading and commenting on his work.

Robina Wright, writing for *Hoofbeats* magazine. April/May 1982

Tom soon realised that Franz was just who was needed to boost Australia's competitive aspirations and gave him lodgings, taught him to drive, and set about finding him more suitable work.

Franz became a regular guest instructor at the Dressage Club, before taking on the appointment of National Coach with the Equestrian Federation (EFA), for which he was nominated by the club. He died in 1978 after making a profound impact on Australian equestrian performance; his training notes were compiled after his death by his wife to produce the book 'Horses were made to be Horses'.

In 1953 and '54 Tom's reputation and profile through his writings led to him being invited to instruct at the first EFA Schools in Western Australia where he introduced dressage and show jumping to this state.

He set a gruelling schedule but one which those who participated remembered with great fondness.

"That first two-week school under Tom's instruction in February 1953 was the start of a new era in horsemanship in Western Australia. Riders came into Perth from all over the state – top polo players, hunting people, stud-masters,

1953, Tom mounted on one of Charlie Readhead's polo ponies in Perth, Western Australia.

teachers, successful show competitors and horsemen and women from the bush...
Tom's stamina and energy seemed boundless – his wife, Pat, says that like many
other horsemen, he was able to 'ride all day and dance all night'."

Robina Wright

In South Australia, Tom's energies also stretched to helping found the
SA Show Jumping Club and he chaired its inaugural meeting. By now,
he had finished duties with the Mounted Division and had more regular
hours as the Commissioner's Orderly at Police Headquarters in Angas
Street. While he declined a position on the Jumping Club committee
Tom offered every support and helped to draft new rules for the sport.

What a busy time for equestrian pursuits in Australia!

The Pony Club movement was just gaining momentum as well, and
Tom saw its guiding principles as being vital to the education of the next
generation of horse custodians. Together with R.M. Williams and
Margaret Clarke, Tom helped to establish South Australia's first, and
Australia's second oldest, Pony Club – the Pegasus Pony Club in 1953.
Tom also taught groups at Gawler River and the Hills based Golden
Spur, which he also encouraged to become Pony Clubs. The Pony Club
Association of South Australia was formed in 1961.

During the years after the formation of the S.A. Association, Tom lectured
and gave demo film evenings to Pony Clubs throughout the State, donating any
fees to the Clubs concerned. When his books were published, copies went to every
State: although not specifically written for Pony Club, everything Tom wrote
was tried and proven and he gives the 'why' as well as 'how'. His four 'Horse
Control' books form the basis of horse-book libraries throughout the country...
The Pony Club Movement brought about one of Tom Roberts' happiest memories
and friendships – getting to know the Chief Instructor of Pony Club, Victoria,
Miss Kay Irving.

Author Unknown

Kay Irving B.A., M.B.E, features in and on the back cover of 'Horse Control – The Rider' and on her visits to South Australia would stay with the Roberts, where talk would last into the small hours.

Where Tom found time to write as well as teach and work is one of life's mysteries. He was clearly a force to be reckoned with! Pat was his greatest supporter, but she too at this time was working and recalls how fond Tom was of staying up to discuss matters with friends.

"Looking back – and me with a full-time secretarial job – I really don't know how I kept up – let alone Tom, nearly 25 years older than I was and there was always a horse, sometimes two, to take out and school before a quick shower, breakfast and drive to the Commissioner's office."

Tom left the Police Force in 1960, but showed no signs of kicking back in retirement. He and Pat bought 'Yundi', a run down 150 acres at Hope Forest, south of Adelaide, and set about restoring it to productivity.

Tom enjoying his retirement at the farm.

Tom demonstrating the essential 'go forward' lesson.

Chapter Six

Moving Forward

During the sixties and seventies, travelling horses to events further afield than riding distance became more accessible for the average horse owner. Many horses, though, had different ideas – getting on a wobbly, noisy dark box to be dragged around by a smelly vehicle was not their idea of fun! Tom was there to help reluctant travellers and had developed a very effective method, one that many horse owners use today, very often oblivious to its origins.

"I remember that I saw him giving horses floating lessons, and it was always very patient. The main thing he was doing was teaching the horse to come up to lead, and there was never, ever any force. He would just put the horse on, and put it off, and put it on, and put it off. He would just do that without upsetting the horse: quite difficult horses, that obviously somebody had tried and messed up. But, again, it all came through to the patience. He didn't care how long it took... Profit you, profit you not."

Pat Hutchens

Tom always used great patience when float training and didn't care how long it took.

In Chapter 20 of 'Horse Control – The Young Horse' Tom thoroughly details 'Loading a Horse on to Transport' and reminds his readers of the value of taking time to do the job well… the capitals are his.

"DO NOT ATTEMPT THIS LOADING LESSON UNLESS YOU HAVE UNLIMITED TIME. "THE MORE YOU HURRY THE LONGER IT TAKES". Allow time – and take all the time you need."

Good advice for any training scenario.

In his later years, due to knee injuries he had sustained lifting ammunition boxes in World War II, Tom was unable to make quick movements but still managed to work successfully with frightened and difficult horses. When he finally couldn't manage to stand without pain, Rita Baker would travel with Tom and do the work with him supervising from his wheelchair.

"You'd just have to stay with them, tapping the whip until the second that they stopped, you stopped. So there was always the reward happening: if it did the right thing, the instant reward was either that it stopped being tapped, or else you patted it or that 'good boy' sort of thing. As soon as they would move forward, or even lean: you might have a horse on the tail gate and even if it would just lean, he would reward it. My goodness, did we have some difficult horses: because, you see, he only got difficult horses. They were the only ones they'd call on you to load; then he'd call on me to load them. There wasn't a horse that ever defeated us, although some were very difficult."

Rita Baker

Tom and Pat had bought an FJ Holden in 1956, registration 3485, which was very close to Tom's World War II army serial number of 3435. She was grey, with a red interior… 'she', because the car was christened 'The Dauntless Dowager' and soon became Tom's trusty chariot as he travelled the state to help horses and riders. The Dowager completed at least three complete turns of the speedo and took Tom and Pat as far afield as Queensland's Atherton Tablelands and often towed two horses up the notorious Willunga Hill on the way to their property.

She was later donated to the Police Historical Society and has been re-purposed as a ceremonial vehicle.

While much of Tom's work with horses was focused on practical fixes for horses with behaviour problems, he was also keen to raise the standard of horsemanship and ensure the safety of riders. He wrote many articles for *Hoofs & Horns* and also began the 'South Australian Rider', a quarterly magazine of the Dressage Club of South Australia. These publications were carefully archived by Pat and Tom, and the articles are nothing short of comprehensive. Here's a small sample of the topics Tom covered:

- Are you going to break him yourself?
- Rugging a wet horse
- Understanding the difficulties of a pupil: Quiet Persistence
- Safety – You and your horse
- The correct sized bridle
- A question for the Judges
- The young horse and traffic
- Does your saddle fit your horse?

You can see, it wasn't all about the horse. Tom also cared for his students and the challenges they faced. Former student, Bernie Biggs, kept a letter Tom wrote to himself and others in 1960, before they started a series of private lessons with him.

It is no use whatever aiming high until you have mastered this SIMPLE thing – Your horse must respond instantly, immediately and with appropriate energy to all pressures of the legs. Having set a pace for him HE MUST MAINTAIN IT without constant goading by the rider. If the rider has to move his legs (increase leg pressure) it should be invisible to an onlooker.

You have to learn to SIT STILL and not urge the horse until he needs it – and THEN make him notice and again SIT STILL. None of you can do this and you must determine to master this trifle… This is the task I set you between this class and the next. Can you produce a horse next time that gives the onlooker the impression that he needs lightly holding rather than constant driving?… Will you have learnt to constantly attend to your horse so that you recognise IMMEDIATELY the slightest change of pace or tempo, then apply the necessary aids? And will you have taught your horse to attend and ACT INSTANTLY on the indications you give? Can you?? We'll see!!

Signed 'Robbie' 5 Feb 1960

Bernie Biggs was one of Robbie's students who was set this challenge. He'd become a devoted student due to the remarkable success of a horse he'd thought had no future. Tom had helped to set them on the right track.

"At the first lesson, I guess like most males of that period, and with what I'd done, we followed around a sort of oblong circle, and Robbie was talking away, and I guess I was bored stiff and a bit pissed off, to be quite honest. The horse I was on, Bobby, jigged all the way and I couldn't get him to settle, because he always wanted to be in front, so went home and wasn't going to go again. But, once again, girlfriend prevailed. Went along next time, and Robbie let me go once again: never had too much to say, and then finally, about halfway through the lesson, he said, 'May I sit on your horse? He's got to walk'. I thought, 'Oh yeah. Smart old bastard', which is how we thought in those days. So he duly climbed on the horse and, low and behold, the horse walked, and the horse did everything he was told. Pat's got the film of that day, and I'm standing there, in the centre, and it's just like a door had been opened. I've got my hand behind my head, incredulous, and I'm thinking, 'I've been half way around Australia, over to India with remounts, rodeo, all this, and all of a sudden this guy could do something I can't.'

I guess this is where that philosophy of Tom Roberts became embedded from that day on: 'It will profit you. It will profit you not'. That's what I walked away with from that lesson. And I guess I was hooked. I was going to sort this horse out once and for all, and that's where it went on; lesson after lesson. Robbie taught me and said, 'That horse will go brilliantly cross country. You've got no troubles'."

Bernie Biggs

Another of Tom's students from this period, Margaret Oliver, uses his techniques to this day and does her best to pass them on to others.

"He used an expression with me 'One – One'. My interpretation is that it refers to equal contact between you and the horse. Between your hand and the horse's mouth. Wherever. When you're leading it: your hand and the contact you have on his nose. It's the equal-ness between you and the horse. It could be one ounce. It might be one pound. It might be whatever you want to call it. If, in your own mind, you have the feel that you are looking for, and you come back to that all the time, you basically show the horse that 'No, that's too heavy. This is what I'm looking for'. If he goes the opposite way, and it's too light, you push him out and encourage him to take it: this is what I'm looking for. I use that ALL the time.

The go forward lesson from the ground: basically teaching them to listen. To stop, to start, to go forward, to go forward with a light tap... Tom Roberts was the first person to introduce the idea of training the horse to understand what the whip taps meant, in order to have a go forward response... These methods are so simple and so effective. To me, to have a horse that goes forward lightly, in hand, i.e. dressage training, means that the horse can do anything. If you teach a horse correctly to start with, you don't have to re-teach it.

He used to say, 'Sit tall. Reach up with the back of your head.' If you can make the back of your head an inch taller, just try it even sitting in your chair, it changes everything. It lifts your spine. It lifts your shoulders. To achieve it your muscle tone is different, so instead of being slouched like a sack of potatoes, you suddenly become tall and erect, and you get a different influence from your back, and you actually sit on your seat bones correctly. Everything just changes from that one simple thing."

Margaret Oliver – student

A young Gill Rolton, who went on to win two Olympic medals, was also taught by Tom Roberts.

*"My main memories of lessons with Robbie are of talking about 'the feel',
and I remember him holding the reins and giving me the feel of what I should
be feeling through the horse's mouth from my hands. It was a light, soft feeling;
not a heavy, hard feeling. It was always a conversation in the connection. That
was the main thing that I took: that I can really remember and that I still use
today when teaching. It's the conversation of the rider with the horse that is
important. It's not domination, it's a conversation.*

*I think that Tom Roberts' legacy is understanding. He was obviously very
gifted as a rider with difficult horses, but he always had a solution to whatever
problem came along. A solution which was not confronting."*

Gill Rolton – Olympian

In 1966 one of Tom's students died in a riding accident. Helen Junge
was a capable horse woman and always advocated the wearing of a
helmet to her riding students. Sadly, she rode her horse one day without
head protection and did not survive a fall. To honour Helen's memory
Tom donated a silver cup he had himself won as a young man in a
footrace in India. The Helen Junge Memorial Trophy was presented
on behalf of the Dressage Club and the Royal Show Society of
South Australia.

It became a perpetual trophy awarded only once to a Young Rider
who has the highest score in the South Australia's annual Novice
Dressage Championship. The rider takes home a silver topped riding
cane to remind them of the importance of wearing protective headgear
every time they ride. The first winner of the Helen Junge Memorial
Trophy was Wayne Copping, who went on to become a sought after
designer and builder of cross country fences for Horse Trials. Many of
the past winners have also gone on to have successful riding careers.

Tom aboard the nervous thoroughbred Why Argue, October 1974.

Chapter Seven

End of Lesson

Tom had always been fascinated with bits – their design, how they worked and why. He collected a vast array and used them in his talks to students. Always an advocate for the horse, Tom's assessment of some bits meant they were preserved only as an item of interest, never to be put in a horse's mouth as they were deemed too severe.

He'd written a series of articles for *Hoofs & Horns* about bits and bitting which had been very well received and Tom had been encouraged to compile these into a book. The timing was good as, by the beginning of the 1970s, Tom's war injuries meant he was increasingly reliant on a wheelchair so his days of standing to teach or train were limited. He could still ride, though, and continued to do so. Into his late 70s Tom was training Dorothy Mansom's latest nervous thoroughbred, Why Argue, and Tom had special mounting blocks made to help him get into the saddle. Once on board, he was secure and made a habit of riding the horse through Adelaide's city squares on public holidays.

Pat stepped into the role of typist and proof reader and brought to the role her good cheer and constructive criticism, as well as providing endless cups of tea (with plenty of sugar!). When 'Horse Control and the Bit' was ready for publication Tom and Pat were told by a publisher that

Tom with Keith Guster with the Helen Junge Memorial Trophy.

they would be lucky to sell a thousand copies. One British publishing house dismissed the manuscript as 'largely irrelevant'. Against all advice, they elected to self-publish and in 1971 Tilbrook Bros. of Clare, produced 5000 copies of the book, a large print run as most independently published books usually started with around 3000 books. Tom was confident his readers would find value in the book, and he was right.

'Horse Control and the Bit' proved very popular and soon sold out. At least ten reprints, with some runs of 5000 copies, were made. The book is a comprehensive study of bits and includes practical advice for the reader on matters such as checking the horse's teeth and how to fit bridles correctly. The information is as relevant today as it was when printed. Today's scientists are only now producing reliable data on the action of bits and bridles. In the lead up to the 2016 Rio Olympics, research was published that showed modern trends with the tightening of nosebands can cause excessive pain. On page 103 of 'Horse Control and the Bit', Tom demonstrates the correct fitting of a cavesson noseband, allowing two fingers to be placed between the horse's nasal plane and the strap. Another recent study discovered that this is now an uncommon practice in competitions, at least, and there are examples of modern nosebands being fastened so tight that the horse's skull is fractured.

In Chapter 11, 'The Port-Mouthed Bit' Tom reveals his belief that he had proven wrong 'the theories of centuries' about this design of this style of bit and its function. He points to this in his Introduction, saying;

"Chapter 11... may, and probably will, provoke a storm of protest at first. But the truth is so manifest, can so clearly be checked and proved, that after the first shock it may be accepted immediately. The full implications are not yet clear. It may well open a new epoch in bit design."

In the decades since Tom wrote this, bit design has certainly moved on, and the array of options is immense. What Tom was getting at with his insight into the actions of the port mouth, was that in all previous work it had been thought that the horse responded more positively to this style of bit because it had a greater, more severe action on the bars of the horse's mouth. It had been thought that the tongue sat neatly into the hollow formed by the port, and thus the 'cannons' of the bit more readily contacted the sensitive bars. Tom had always made good use of equine skeletons he sourced from a friend at the Adelaide Zoo, where horses are still used to feed the carnivores, and he clearly spent some time looking at skulls and various bits. What he reveals about the port mouth is that, in fact, the tongue is compressed and thus acts as a cushion for the bit and protects the bars.

"The really important fact is that a port mouthpiece makes the Bit milder and less punishing in many ways, and that all the advantages and perhaps more – extend to the Pelham. The facts are as they have always been; it is our knowledge and theories that have been in error."

While today's scientists investigate bits and their effects with the tools science now offers, how a bit feels to an individual horse inside his mouth is still a best guess. Professor Hilary Clayton of Michigan State University has studied bits with real time fluoroscopy x-rays and when asked about Tom's theories responded with her personal opinion:

"You ask a good question and I don't have a definitive answer. It would need a 3D reconstruction to answer your question and that's difficult to do because data would need to be collected with the horse conscious and standing with normal muscle tone in the tongue.

Based on personal experience rather than research data, I agree that the tongue often forms a cushion between the bit and the bars and this effect may not be limited to ported bits. If you part the horse's lips, even with a jointed snaffle you can often see the tongue bulging over the bars and appearing to have a cushioning effect."

Professor Hilary Clayton

This matter of the horse's comfort and what he saw as previously erroneous thinking was clearly important to Tom and, along with his evolution of the loading methods, are the main innovations for which he hoped he might be remembered.

Interestingly, also in the same book Tom ponders whether one day the design of saddle trees might be improved by dispensing with the front and rear arches that can occasionally cause discomfort. He suggests that moulded fibreglass might be a solution, and almost fifty years later one of Australia's leading saddlers has launched just that 'revolutionary' make of tree.

As his first book had been so successful, Tom was encouraged to pen his second in the series. 'Horse Control – The Young Horse', published in 1974, set out his experience for starting the education of young horses. While Tom always advised that this job was best left to professionals he was aware that many amateur owners, and particularly young women, would always be keen to take on this task themselves. He wanted to make the process as safe as possible for humans and the most humane it could be for horses.

"Tom's clear, natural style gives the impression that he is right there talking to his pupil. This, and his insight into the limited mind of the horse, makes him a most convincing teacher in print."

Robina Wright 1984 from an article entitled
'Tom Roberts – Grand Old Horseman'

This second volume was also soon sold out and its popularity necessitated at least eight print runs of around 10,000 copies each. People from all walks of life and from all over the world who shared Tom's fascination with horses saw great value in his words. Letters of appreciation were carefully catalogued and each responded to by Tom and Pat.

In 1977 Tom began work on the third book 'The Rider', the publications now easily recognizable by their distinctive yellow covers and concise layout. Tom made certain that he used 'real life' photographs of his pupils' training so that the contents were encouraging for all readers. This book has a number of photos of Erica Taylor training Crown Law, a horse she bred and broke in herself and on which she represented Australia as an individual rider in Dressage at the 1988 Seoul Olympic Games.

"I've often said that there's not been one thing that Robbie told me that I've felt wasn't right. You know, years later when I'd progressed to a much higher standard (and trained with international instructors), there has never been one thing when I've thought, 'Well, Robbie was wrong'. Never, ever, one thing that he wasn't right about.

Robbie was a constant through all my horses. I can remember him when we used to have dressage in town on Pulteney St... the Dressage Club used to run competitions there, and I remember Robbie was there one day, and he was about 70 then, I reckon, and I might have had Crown Law there as a young horse, and I clearly remember, because I was quite taken aback, he said, 'Erica, when you get to my age you'll be better than I was'. I was quite astounded, and thinking, 'I'll probably never get to your age, let alone ever be as good'.

He wasn't afraid to give a compliment. I never heard him put anyone down. He was always encouraging. Always.

I never heard him mention harmony but, in hindsight, it was about the rider being intelligent enough to be able to teach the horse. Which is really what it's down to. If the rider hasn't got the brains to get through to the horse what he wants, the poor horse hasn't got much hope. I keep saying to people, 'Dressage is so simple', and they look at me in amazement. But it is. It is so simple, as long as you get the basics right."

Erica Taylor

When Erica was selected for the 1986 World Dressage Championships Pat and Tom contributed $1000 to the cost of her trip and wrote to wish her and William (Crown Law) well, reminding Erica that "not one of the top German riders had such a beautiful piaffe as those William does for you". The Roberts were generous with sponsorship of events and riders.

During the writing of 'The Rider' Tom had to be hospitalised due to an infection in his war damaged knees, and he was not expected to survive. He spent twelve months in hospital and as soon he was able, continued working on his manuscript, with Pat by his side. Letters flooded in from around the world with best wishes for the recovery of their favourite equestrian author. This third volume was published in 1980 and once well enough, Tom carried on his lectures and his interest expanded to donkeys.

He'd been invited to open the 1979 National Donkey Seminar and the admiration its members developed for Tom led to the NSW Society adopting his phrase "Go forward, dear" as its motto. Tom's new found appreciation of the donkey's survival skills and its trainability extended to his pondering their evolutionary niche and adaptations.

"Only in very recent years have I been interested in them and I would like to know a lot more about them. It is never sufficient for us to note to ourselves, 'That's odd'; we should always go a little further and find out, 'How come?'."

In 1982 Tom's adopted country awarded him with the Medal of the Order of Australia (OAM) 'for services to equestrian sport.' He travelled to Government House in the Dauntless Dowager which, by special permission, was parked inside the grounds for the ceremony.

The trusty FJ continued active service transporting Tom, wearing his trademark black hat, to lectures and running cartons of books from where they were stored in an old stable to Port Adelaide for shipping around the world. Tom and Pat's home at Richmond had previously been the site of a thoroughbred stud and it is happily remembered by his grandchildren for its horses, roses and Daphne, the former hurdy-gurdy horse which had pride of place on the verandah.

In 1984, 'Reminiscences' was published after requests from Tom's friends. The memories, anecdotes and illustrations are a wealth of historical and practical information shared with characteristic generosity and humility.

Tom had started work on compiling his war diaries into a publication, but after a short illness passed away in 1989, a few weeks before his birthday. Family, students and friends mourned his loss but took comfort in the legacy he had left. Pat had kept the many letters of condolence and personal notes acknowledging his influence.

He lived a full life of interest and achievement; he was a man of original thought and innovation. He never turned aside from a plea for help or advice – whether for humans or horses; and he fought hard for the rights of the 'ordinary man'. A man of great integrity and kindness.

Obituary – Author unknown

Tom Robert's legacy is there for all horses and the people who work with them. He might be pleased to see his life's work demonstrated in the calm footsteps of the horse loading for the first time, or in the relaxed snort riders instinctively recognise as reward for their sensitive encouragement. Perhaps it is also seen in the jumping horse responding athletically in the Olympic arena or in the trail rider confidently approaching unfamiliar terrain. These are the little things that add up to a safe and harmonious ride, and Tom knew how much they mattered.

Amongst the substantial collection of clippings and records that were shared with the authors by the Roberts family and Pat's relatives were these telling, unsourced, paragraphs. We think they do better than any we could construct to close this part of Tom's book:

Tom was always very conscious of the difficulties that faced the horse during his education.

A lot of people think it's natural for the horse to stop if you hurt him in the mouth – but to go faster if you hurt him anywhere else… they should read Tom's books…

I can remember him so often saying, "There are a thousand things the horse can try that are not what you want. You must be patient, for he is trying. How dare you punish him when he is trying? Think kindly, think, 'Not that… not that, dear'. And don't forget the dear!"

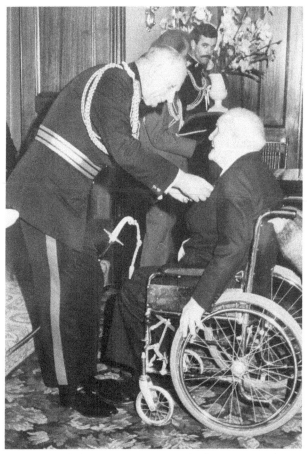

Tom receiving his Medal of the Order of Australia for services to equestrian sport.

Tom had great empathy and compassion for both horses and humans.

Part 2

Tom Roberts, his Methods

by Dr Andrew McLean

Tom Roberts.

Introduction

Tom Roberts, the horse trainer, gave a wealth of training information to so many people throughout his lifetime, both in his personal instructions and in his books. But aside from the precise horse training instructions and his visionary understanding of horse training, Tom Roberts the man is also remembered for his undiscriminating empathy and compassion. Tom loved people as much as he did horses. He wanted to work with the horse's nature and as much with the human's nature so that together these two could intertwine in a positive and meaningful way. His writings echo those of other great horseman of the past: good horsemanship should include nothing artificial and should reflect what is best in both horse and human nature. Horse trainers would do well to consider Tom's approach to his horses and his students. Above all, he was an exemplary human being and was known far and wide for it. He was not the trainer or coach who would humiliate people no matter how long their journey in horsemanship was going to take. It is really not possible to claim to have compassion for horses while having none for fellow human beings. He was always kind to people whom he described as 'still finding their way'.

Even when it came to necessary criticism of someone's technique with horses, Tom would find an encouraging way to get the message across, and this was in the times when criticism of students was a normal thing. Tom was ahead of his time in so many ways. In all of the statements and interviews with those who remember him, Tom's encouraging and caring manner shine through continuously.

"Go forward, dear!" may seem a rather old fashioned title these days. However, the title of this book could be nothing other than that, because "Go forward, dear!" embodies Tom in all his interactions with horses and people. Tom believed that if you include the word "dear" in all your

requests, it will diminish any anger that may be present due, if nothing else, to frustration. Training can be frustrating at times and people who are easily frustrated have less success. Framing your requests as polite, respectful ones of both horse and rider will put you in the rightful place of trainer rather than despot, autocrat or master and it will help your requests to become more ethical and what's more, effective.

My interest in Tom Robert's work came well before I had made any significant journey into the science of training. I came from a family of horse-riding people; my mother was a successful show rider while my grandfather was successful jumper at the beginning of the 20th century in central Queensland. I spent my childhood in rural Victoria and my youth on King Island in Bass Strait where horses were heavily intertwined with our lives. In fact, animals formed the most important elements of my childhood and this led me to become a zoologist. Early in my career I taught zoology part time at the University of Tasmania in Launceston and at the same time I began my journey in eventing. I became curious to see how I could improve my horse's training by knowing more about animal learning and this led to me undertaking my PhD in equine cognition and learning.

For many years beginning in the late 1980s I would conduct training clinics throughout Australia. This soon expanded to the point where I would conduct up to four three-day clinics in each Australian state and eventually in New Zealand, the USA, Canada and Europe. When I went to South Australia, one of Pat Roberts's friends, Natalie Chisholm, came to observe my clinic. Natalie came up to me at the end and said she saw Tom's work in mine, and that we had some similarities as men and in our empathetic approach to both people and horses. She suggested and arranged that next time I came to Adelaide, I should visit Pat. So I did that and was very warmly welcomed. I went to see her many times and each visit Pat would have the 8mm movie projector ready to roll and we would have tea and biscuits. I learned so much from those movies. The scene was made even more extraordinary because Pat would do the voice-over to accompany the movies, explaining in detail what Tom was saying at the time or doing. I got to know Tom through these experiences with Pat as well as from his writing. I'll never forget her animation in showing me her taking the first ride on a horse that the elderly Tom had broken in, and there she was on board this slightly tense horse in a long flowing yellow dress, red high heels, diamanté winged glasses and of course, no riding hat. The indomitable 1950s FJ Holden in the background completed the picture of horse training in the yesteryears.

Tom always opted for the gentle approach, always sought lightness yet did not sacrifice obedience for it, and most of all, he knew the principles of training and taught very well with the use of pressure and release. As I read Tom's books, the big question that kept occurring to me was, "How did he come to know so many details of animal learning?" It's easy to say that, like many horsemen, he had such a diverse and strong background in his cavalry training but there is far more to the extent of Tom's insights. Many horsemen alive today have had vast experience but I know of none who compare with Tom in theoretical knowledge that aligns with animal learning processes. Tom was a humble man who had a deep respect for Australia's first National Dressage Coach, Franz Mairinger. Franz was a consummate horseman and trainer but Tom's background was far more diverse and exploratory. Franz held Tom in high regard and, on more than one occasion, he wrote to him asking for his solution to behaviour problems that he couldn't solve. Their correspondence, including the letters of appreciation from Franz, are archived along with the rest of Tom's paraphernalia.

The Science of Training

As I have already mentioned, Tom had an understanding of the science behind horse training. It was probably an unconscious comprehension and it was tempered by his compassion. He may not have known it but, in the way he approached training, Tom was a scientist and a very good one. Welfare and effectiveness are inseparable. When you are young you tend to learn and do things in any endeavour in ways that you first found appealing. You emulate other people and do your best to learn from them. In the horse world many great horsemen have learned this way, by emulating and learning from one particular individual. Some young people, and there seems to be more of them now than ever, cherry-pick training techniques from many trainers and so they constantly shift from one trainer to another. It rarely works for them in the long term because they don't have the background or education to understand the overall structure of the training of any one of the trainers they take a little from. They don't know what they don't know.

There is no single way that things should be done and there are many methods that are successful. However, how you measure success is significant. In horse training, if you measure success purely in terms of outcome then those training practices that result in the extravagant movement of horses ridden in hyperflexion or with shortened necks, where the nasal plane is behind the vertical, come at the expense of the horse's welfare. What is needed is an optimal mix of good welfare and training effectiveness and this is essentially what Tom proposed.

Training is synonymous with learning: good training is simply where the trainer utilises learning processes. The better you do it, the more efficient the training. Therefore, when training is perfectly aligned with the animal's natural behaviours and learning processes, then there can be no greater efficiency in training because training is learning. To repeat, horse training is always enhanced by an optimal utilisation of the animal's natural learning systems. The International Society for Equitation Science (ISES) maintains (see www.equitationscience.com/learning-theory-in-equitation) a number of training principles that horse trainers should adhere to from the welfare viewpoint:

Training Principle 1 – Take into account the horse's ethology and cognition

Training Principle 2 – Use learning theory appropriately

Training Principle 3 – Train easy-to-discriminate cues

Training Principle 4 – Shape responses and movements

Training Principle 5 – Elicit responses one-at-a-time

Training Principle 6 – Train only one response per signal

Training Principle 7 – Form consistent habits

Training Principle 8 – Train persistence of responses (self-carriage)

Training Principle 9 – Avoid and dissociate flight responses

Training Principle 10 – Demonstrate minimum levels of arousal sufficient for training

It is remarkable and interesting to compare Tom's training with these ISES principles. This is the chief focus in this section of *Go forward, dear* because there is no better way to analyse the correctness and accuracy of any training. As you will see, even by comparison with today's trainers who live in a time where they do have access to this information (Equitation Science officially arose in 2005), Tom's training aligned consistently well with these principles and a great deal better than that of many contemporary trainers.

These ISES training principles are updated from time to time as new evidence emerges from research. Thus in writing this section of the book, I have highlighted and compared the chief elements of each of the ten principles.

Movement Needs

An important hard-wired aspect of the horse's behaviour pattern is his need for movement. Horses are born with the need to move from 7 to 18 km per day, and the stress that rises from thwarting this creates increased restlessness. Confined horses show an increased likelihood of explosive activity when opportunities arise. So when the stabled horse is removed from the stable he might have a burst of leaping, running and bucking.

In behavioural science, the sudden energy an animal shows when it is released from confinement is known as 'post inhibitory rebound'. Horses in stables without adequate exercise are prone to this, however the deeper problem that is widely unknown to horse owners is that the thwarting of this drive to move creates a level of insecurity that can contribute to active and passive coping mechanisms (conflict behaviours and 'shutting down') and stereotypies such as weaving. Similar behaviours are seen in many other animals when their natural behaviours are curtailed – think of the tiger pacing his cage or the elephant rocking from one foot to another.

The horse's need for movement and the consequences of inadequate exercise were frequently described by Tom as a constant source of behaviour problems and general malcontent in the horse. Tom recognised that the more boxed up or yarded a horse is, the more likely he will *"let off steam"* on a ride out. He advised, *"Turn them loose in a paddock, no matter how small, whenever that is possible and even a very short stay there is better than a day in a small yard"* he advised. And, *"allow at least 10 minutes for him to calm down after his frolicking"*.

Social Needs

Like all social animals, the horse also has a strong need for company. Whereas our knowledge of attachment theory was first known only with respect to the mother-infant bond, it later extended to include relationships between people generally and later again to define relationships between humans and companion animals such as dogs. It was discovered that dogs, like humans, upon reuniting with their humans experience a spike of endorphins and oxytocin. Tom was an advocate of a very gradual weaning approach where the foal would be briefly removed from his mother and then reunited before the foal became anxious and then gradually lengthen the periods of time away from the dam *"and after a while, the foal ceases to worry"* (about being away from his mother).

Isolation has been described, in humans at least, as the single most underpinning factor in mental disorders and it has even been shown to be significant in addiction behaviours. It is therefore not surprising that horses, too, suffer from isolation. The increased need for allogrooming (grooming each other) upon reuniting horses or even taking their rugs off is understood to be the effect of the soothing touch to increase levels of security. Horses are still the only known species where the scratching or raking of teeth on the wither region, neck and back is known to significantly lower heart rate.

Tom was an advocate of caressing the horse on the neck rather than patting as a reward. *"Rub him and scratch him,"* Tom advised. Yet patting is commonplace, not only in horse training but also with dog trainers and mahouts who prefer patting rather than caressing their elephants. Horses and dogs far prefer stroking and rubbing to patting and my experience with elephants makes it abundantly clear to me that elephants also prefer caressing, especially on the bulbous forehead region. Patting, when you stop and think about it, is not very distinct from punishment. For example, how is a horse meant to know the difference between the slap on the neck an excited rider gives for a good performance and the smack it receives if it tries to bite?

Grazing Needs

Another instinctive, hard-wired behaviour in animals is the foraging drive. For horses this is the need to spend a large amount of time, on average thirteen hours per day, eating low quality herbage. For many domestic horses however this is not fulfilled. Instead, with the best of human intentions, the horse may be fed a few high quality meals per day and then spend the rest of the time doing little or nothing and so it is not unexpected that that the horse can develop the stereotypy known as cribbing, popularly attributed to boredom. It is well worth considering that it's not just that the horse likes to eat for over half a day, but that mentally he needs to do this. Thwarting this, as with all of the other drives, lowers the horse's feeling of security and contributes to active and passive coping mechanisms. Tom's years in the light horse cavalry made him acutely aware of the horse's need for roughage and time spent just eating. Tom's views on feeding were quite different from the attitudes of today where we are blinded by profit-driven feed companies to over-feed concentrated cereal-based feeds to horses in favour of roughage. He especially believed that feeding grain to young horses is problematic: *"A young horse should not be doing enough work to utilise grain foods – concentrates."*

Clarity in Communication Needs

Behavioural science recognises the importance of what is known as predictability and controllability and these needs are hard-wired in animals; mismatches contribute very strongly to active and passive coping mechanisms. Predictability is the need to establish certain markers that are signs of good things such as food or bad things such as the arrival of predators. For example, the feral horse might associate certain landscape features with favoured grazing patches, and certain signs in mares are a green light for stallions to mate.

On the other hand, a particular birdcall might herald the arrival of a predator and, more individually, certain behaviours in horses, such as pinned ears, might herald imminent aggression over a resource. In fact, throughout the horse's entire life he adds to his innate predictive list of triggers of certain behaviours through learning. The learning processes themselves I will discuss a little later as another broad principle of training, however it is important to recognise that while the earlier behavioural needs were totally hard-wired, learning processes can be seen also as a hard-wired framework within which the gaps are filled by experience.

Controllability is about the animal learning to respond to the cues in his environment and also being able to communicate effectively with other animals in his world. Learning these cues ultimately ensure his comfort and survival. So controllability is very much about the horse learning to successfully respond to other horses (as well as other animals and objects) and to successfully cause other animals to respond to threats or other cues.

So even going on a trail ride incorporates myriad signs given by the surrounding topography and animal life to the horse; to step over, or around, or on, certain terrain features and the successful locomotion reinforces security through predictability and controllability. The horse learns that trees are unchangeably solid and puddles can be stepped in or over. These things seem so obvious as to hardly be worth mentioning yet the building of an animal's security and confidence hinges upon his successful navigation of his physical and behavioural world.

As horse trainers, we tap into the horse's needs for predictability and controllability. The absolute necessity of giving the light aid before any stronger pressure when the horse is non-compliant is an example of predictability. All cues, body postures, seat and voice are important because they confer security. Studies on dogs where they had to jump from one electrified compartment to another non-electrified one showed very clearly, even when they could escape the shock, how disturbed the dogs became when there was no warning sign that the floor would be electrified. When, in another part of the experiment, a buzzer sounded before the electricity was turned on, the dogs jumped to the other compartment and were secure and calm in their ability to predict and control the aversive situation. When the predictable cues were made to be unreliable, the dogs suffered far worse mental degradations than they did even when the grid floors were electrified without any warning signs because at least they could escape. Through his books, Tom recognised the importance of the light aid and the great significance of training that is clear to the horse. *"Failure to keep the young horse light in hand can give much trouble later on… Feel at your end what is happening at his"*.

The core of Tom's message was captured in his words: *"Do not deceive yourself: the horse's faults indicate the degree of his trainer's failure. Every vice, every bad habit he learns or acquires, has to be laid at the door of the person who, by lack of knowledge or care perhaps, permitted him to gain that harmful experience"*.

Mental Abilities

Another core element of the ISES principles of training concerns the horse's cognition or mental capabilities. To be effective, the training of any species requires knowledge of the animal's mental strengths and limitations. In general terms, the brains of mammals are remarkably similar and operations of the various brain parts are very consistent. The major difference between humans and horses lies in the workings of the front part of the brain, known as the prefrontal cortex. The prefrontal cortex is the major area for reasoning and holding images and thoughts in our heads when the event that produced them has long passed. Some psychologists call this our global workspace. It is like a giant stage where we can imagine the effect of a behaviour before we actually do it. The neural cells of the human prefrontal cortex are far more dense than those of all other animals and they appear, microscopically, far more granular. Dolphins and chimps come closest to us in this department. It is this brain region in human evolution that has flourished because our survival depended on out-smarting both our predators and our prey.

In terms of cell type horses are deficient in this area. This means that they most likely have difficulty thinking ahead and back and that they 'live in the moment'. Most importantly it means that, as horse trainers, we should be careful not to assume that horses necessarily *understand* their training or that they know what they have just done when the behaviour has finished. Tom was unique amongst horseman in that he seemed to realise this, *"He seems to be quite unable to think ahead like we do,"* and, *"He is conscious only of what he is experiencing now"*. Punishing horses as if they know what they have done wrong is commonplace in the horse world yet it is futile and unethical. The same is true for delayed rewards.

Punishment can only work if it is connected in time (i.e. without a break) to the behaviour which the trainer wishes to decrease. If disconnected punishment worked then hitting a horse for knocking a rail would teach him to be a cleaner jumper but that most certainly isn't the case. Tom was adamant in saying that, *"Punishment and teaching are divorced"*.

In terms of strengths, the horse has an outstanding memory. People often remark at the memory of the elephant but there is every reason to suspect that the memory of the horse is as good. What we do know is the horse has a very good recognition memory, which is a memory for triggers of behaviours, but not the kind of human 'videographic' memory of the entire event. This requires a far more extensive and dense prefrontal cortex and isn't necessary for the horse in any sense of its adaptations. Such a memory, known as a recall memory, is helpful for predators for such activities as ambush (i.e. when you need to know that the animal is there but can't see it) and for tool users or animals whose food is patchy (to save wasted foraging journeys). But it is of little use for horses because on top of it all, such flexible abilities are expensive to maintain and a grazing diet just doesn't provide enough fuel.

What serves the grazing prey animal very well is an accurate recognition memory. The superiority of the horse's recognition memory over ours is remarkable. Every rider or horse handler soon finds out that the horse noticed the bucket that wasn't there the day before, yet the human, with supposedly superior mental sophistication, hardly notices it.

Tom seemed to have a very clear understanding of the horse's mental strengths and limitations. He admonishes the use of punishment continuously in his writing and stresses the importance of timing of the aids. He notes how futile it is to attempt to punish or reward a response when it is too late.

Tom even realised that the horse doesn't extrapolate signals from one side of its body to the other. *"The young horse sees things when going around right-handed, say and settles down after a turn or two; but change direction and move around the other way and he has to inspect and accept everything afresh."*

Learning

Another of the ISES principles implores trainers to learn about the basics of equine learning processes and apply them correctly.

Negative Reinforcement

Horses are excellent at learning through negative reinforcement. This learning process is largely misunderstood as meaning that it is about applying something negative or that it is the same as punishment. Neither of these is true. Negative reinforcement is the removal (hence the mathematical meaning of negative) of something the horse finds aversive such as the rider's rein or leg pressure. This removal increases the likelihood of that behaviour in the future. So, when a rider closes their fingers on the reins and this pressure is immediately softened when the horse slows then the horse will soon learn to slow reliably because he has learned that the reaction of slowing means the pressure will go away: *"The pressure on the reins should be lightened immediately, if only for a moment. Try to tell him through the reins, 'That's the idea, that will profit you!'"*

The horse learns all the basic reactions in equitation in this way. He learns to accelerate via the rider's leg pressure, he learns to decelerate via the rein pressure on the mouth; he learns to turn and change direction through the release of pressure on a single rein and to turn his hindquarters through the release of the pressure of the rider's single leg. These are the basics in all horse sports. It is the refinement of these basics throughout the horse's life that is the chief focus of his education. In the early stages of the horse's education it is the shrinkage of the pressures to very light versions of the aids. Next he learns to acquire other associated cues such as seat, posture or voice that are connected with these leg and rein aids.

Tom's deep knowledge of the workings of negative reinforcement is perhaps his greatest achievement. Very few, if any, authors have so accurately encapsulated negative reinforcement as clearly as he has in his dictum "profit you, profit you not". This is truly remarkable since negative reinforcement is the major learning process of horse training. His most illuminating description of negative reinforcement is seen in his famous 'pin' analogy: He would ask his pupils, *"Why do you jump up instantly if you sit on an upturned tack or drawing pin?"* People would answer, *"Because it hurts,"* and Tom would reply, *"No, you jump up not because it hurts, but to stop it hurting!"* The horse learns to stop and go in the same way. Throughout Tom's books, he constantly refers to the importance of removing the pressure: lightening the pressure of rein and leg when the horse offers the correct response. Similarly with the whip, instead of viewing it as a punishment tool he promoted the deft use of negative reinforcement where the whip is used in a rhythmic tapping motion that stops as soon as the desired response is achieved: *"Move forward. If you don't then the whip will tap and worry you until you do – then it stops".*

In times past, all of the texts that have been written focus on how to ride a horse but not how to train one. In fact, Tom lamented this also: *"Only too often the top exponents of the art of dressage can produce the effects aimed for, can teach their horses and then with the aid of the trained horse can teach others.*

But most of them do not attempt to explain 'how' and 'why' the effect is produced. They themselves learned without a lot of explanation: they learned to DO – not to talk. They were taught WHAT but not WHY."

Tom correctly applied his "profit you, profit you not" to all interactions with horses, not just the use of the reins and legs. He explained how horses become head-shy in these terms because it is the removal of the human hand that profits the horse in this case: *"…keep your hand (on his head) and follow his head around with your hand until he lowers it to your hand. Which he will do eventually." "When he does – show him 'that will profit you' and quietly move your hand away again. Rest. And then start again from the beginning".*

Positive Reinforcement

Positive reinforcement is a simple concept; it's all about rewarding a behaviour. The horse does something you want, like lifting his leg, and you give him a food treat or a caress. To be effective, however, there is more to it. The reward must be given the instant the correct response is offered. Failing that, a 'marker' can be used that tells the animal that a reward is coming. The marker must be unique and it must *always* predict the onset of the reward. That means when the marker is used, such as a clicker or (as in zoos) a high pitched whistle, 'payment' must follow in the form of a real reward. For example, "good boy" can be used to herald a caress or food, most typically. Once the trainer has taught a horse the value of 'good boy' through this pairing then it should always be followed by the positive reinforcer, otherwise it will lose its value and pleasing association.

Many people believe that simply praising the horse is intrinsically rewarding but this is unlikely because there isn't anything naturally rewarding about praise. Praise is like money. Receiving money is great so long as you can do something with it, and it's great because you can do something with it. However, if money had no value at all, it would not be so rewarding to receive it. So money is rewarding because it symbolises something that is rewarding. When praise is associated with the release of pressure, and especially if it comes *before* the release of pressure, it can come to be associated with it, if the trainer is careful to maintain this contingency. Throughout Tom's writings, he was constantly encouraging people to praise horses when the correct response is offered. Praise is usually used with a soothing voice and it should be pointed out that talking in a soothing voice, while not necessarily rewarding, may be calming and is always a good thing. Tom advocated the use of a 'purring' voice: *"When he tends to do right or to do better, change to a purring voice type of sound….. and let him let him associate that kind of sound with your end of lesson reward."*

It is fascinating to note that the major work of the behaviourists (scientists studying the mechanics of learning) in the post Second World War period was also the time that Tom was beginning to formulate his own views on horse training. Although he didn't elaborate in his books about the use of positive reinforcement with food treats, he was very much ahead of his time in the use of tactile reinforcement which is seen more in his films than in his writing except for his encouragement for horse people to *"rub and scratch"* the young horse. Those who worked with Tom directly have told us that he was fond of using a milk thistle plant, which horses find very tasty, as a reward or to make a positive association when they were showing some difficulties with a task.

At the time of his writing, 'attachment theory' was emerging and the Western world was reeling from the seemingly cold-hearted approach of the neobehaviourist doctrine that is encapsulated in B.F Skinner's belief that man is essentially a machine: he behaves in lawful, predictable ways in response to external stimuli. The result of this doctrine was an approach to rearing children in a no-nonsense way, where parents and care-givers were encouraged to prioritise the child's conditioning. The absence of love was the chief argument and weapon of Skinner's opponents and from this grew a major force of opposition to neobehaviourism. Their proof was that experiments done mostly by Harry Harlow on motherless rhesus monkeys showed the devastating effects on children deprived of love and also the 'hospitalisation effect'; that children raised in orphanages run on Skinnerian loveless principles were dying like flies and after months of deprivation in these institutions would never be able to be normally adjusted human beings.

What Bowlby and Ainsworth famously showed at the end of the 1960s was the importance of love and its effect via touch. Touch, as we now know, is critical in the establishment of positive attachments and the development of security and confidence. This has now been shown to not only include mother to infant but also to define all close human relationships and more recently to define human-companion animal (such as dogs) relationships. There is growing evidence that attachment theory provides at least some of the explanation of the human-horse bond. Touch is therefore an essential component of our relationships with horses that is not only provided by caressing but also via grooming, massage and other interventions. While the majority of horse people patted horses, Tom rewarded by caressing and perhaps, without necessarily knowing it, he created schedules of secondary reinforcement with soothing words and praise connected to the caress. He frequently advocated the use of praise and tactile reward when the horse responded correctly to negative reinforcement.

Punishment

Tom advised, *"The use of force and pain is not necessary"*. Punishment is technically defined in two ways, positive and negative. Positive punishment is *the addition of something the horse doesn't like* to reduce a behaviour whereas negative punishment is *the removal of something the horse does like* also to reduce a behaviour. So positive punishment can be seen in the example where the horse kicks and gets a smack for it. The human hopes to reduce the behaviour of kicking in the future.

As I mentioned earlier, for punishment to work it must be physically connected in time to the behaviour it is meant to reduce. There are significant problems associated with positive punishment in terms of the relationship of the person doing the punishing and the animal on the receiving end. Moreover, it has been shown that punished animals may experience learning problems as well as effects on physical health.

Negative punishment has fewer problems. An example of negative punishment is where the horse is pawing when tethered and the person walks away, i.e. the human removes himself and this diminishes the attention paid to the horse in order to reduce the pawing. This is the same technique teachers use in kindergartens where the child that kicks another child is removed and placed in the 'naughty corner' in the hope that the aggression will disappear.

Tom constantly implores horse people to recognise the negative effects of punishment. Punishment, he said, *"should be reserved for exceptional occasions. Don't think reward and punishment"*, instead think, *"encourage and discourage"* through his profit you – profit you not theme. Tom goes further to say, *"Above all things, we must be most tolerant when he tries something other than what we have in mind. When he tries to do other than what we want of him when we begin to teach him this or any other lesson, on no account should we punish him. We must assume that he is trying to find out what we want him to do."*

Classical Conditioning & Lightness

Classical conditioning is also known as Pavlovian conditioning because it was Pavlov who first noticed the association that animals make when some cue or event is reliably connected with another already known or inbuilt response. Pavlov showed that if he rang a bell before a dog was presented with food, soon the ringing of the bell would produce salivation. Later researchers showed that in other positive reinforcement situations, any cue that regularly occurred beforehand would be learned as a predictor of that reward. Since then, studies have shown that any cue that predicts any event is acquired along the same neural pathways and this accounts for the uptake of a light aid in equitation because it is predictive of a stronger pressure and enables the animal to learn to avoid the stronger pressure by responding to the light aid first. Soon the horse responds to the light aid alone because it predicts the strongest pressure. Tom was well aware of this association and noted that: *"With repetition he will come to associate the seat movement with the demands of your legs, and it is then for the rider to progressively diminish the strength of his ordinary leg aids until eventually the horse responds to the changes of seat pressures alone."*

Tom called the smooth increase from a light rein aid to a stronger aid 'stretching the rein': *"Take teaching the horse to stop as an instance, imagine you are walking at, say, 4 miles an hour and you slightly stretch the reins to ask the horse to stop. He isn't yet clear what the tighten reins means and instead of stopping, he moves his jaw or his head, or for a while resists the bit or 'drops it' but continues at 4 miles per hour. The rider quietly persists with the stretched rein. After a few paces, finding that what he has done or is doing has not profited him in any way, the horse may either by accident or design try going slower. He drops to 3 miles per hour. You lighten the reins again."*

This prediction is not necessarily conscious, it is more likely at the subconscious level and soon the response to the light aid becomes a habit. Tom was a staunch advocate of lightness and he was well aware of the importance of the light aid arriving first. Referring to alterations of body posture, Tom explained that *"the tiniest movement of the rider's bodyweight can become an aid"* and *"All aids should be as light as possible"*.

Habituation

Habituation is a learning process that basically describes how animals become accustomed to things in the environment. As Charles Darwin pointed out two centuries ago, animals evolved to live and eat in their habitats as efficiently as possible. The importance of this is that there is competition in the living world. Grazing animals like horses have to compete not only with other ungulates for grass but, for example, with the millions of insects that also eat grass. So the most efficient way that grazing can be done with a minimum of effort means that those particular animals that possess these life enhancing qualities will pass on their efficiency to future generations. Habituation is one of those efficiencies. It is a waste of time running away from every unfamiliar thing in your environment. You should only run away from those things that are definitely dangerous. So, after a period of time, animals learn to diminish their reactions to stimuli that pose no threat. Habituation explains why horses that live next to railway lines soon don't show any reaction at all when trains pass. The word desensitisation refers to the techniques that trainers might use to desensitise horse to stimuli.

Tom used the term 'old hat' to refer to the situation where the horse learns to form the habit you want rather than react to a new or unfamiliar environment by what behavioural scientists know as systematic desensitisation: *"If you are taking the horse to a show for the first time, get on him when you are there and move around for only a few minutes. Then put him away again. The thing is to leave in his mind the thought: "There's nothing to it". If a sight, sound, situation, company, condition, demand or anything at all, is novel – it will lose its fearfulness more quickly if you terminate it before anything has a chance to go wrong. It becomes 'Old Hat'."*

Shaping

Shaping is the progressive building of a particular behaviour from the most basic attempt to the final product. Tom was not alone in his imploring his pupils to take their time and gradually shape their desired responses. He implored riders to *"Introduce one thing at a time"*. Among the Old Masters, the most noted advice in this area comes from Gustav Steinbrecht who declared that training should not be rushed and each step should *"...all follow one another in such a way that the preceding exercise always constitutes a secure basis for the next one. Violations of this rule will always exert payment later on; not only by a triple loss of time but very frequently by resistances, which for a long time if not forever interfere with the relationship between horse and rider"*.

For example, when you first train a totally naive horse to go forward, you will find he of course has no idea. Through negative reinforcement of leg pressure the horse learns to go forward but he may be sluggish, drifting sideways and may stall shortly after, among other things that could go wrong. So the concept of shaping demands that you target just one aspect first then another and then another. When training the horse to go forward under saddle, Tom advised that with all gaits, *"Each time you ask for it and obliges, let him know immediately, 'That's right'."*

Similarly, in training the horse to lead, Tom explained: *"The first lesson is to teach him to step forward one STEP, no matter how small"*. When training the go forward response, there are quite a few shaping steps along the way. First you might reward the horse for taking the tiniest step in the correct direction, and then taking a complete step, then rewarding the continuation of the steps and then for maintaining line and direction.

Tom would explain throughout his writing that things should be done gradually and never to overload the horse with too many things. For example, in teaching the horse to load into a float/trailer, Tom writes, *"Prepare the horse for loading by getting him accustomed to the sight, sound and feel of a wooden surface before you attempt to load him"*. In teaching the horse flying changes, Tom recognised the context-specific nature of horses (they tend to do the same things in the same places) in tandem with shaping and suggests riding the horse in canter along the diagonal line of the arena and when you come to the corner, *"make a simple change of lead there in the corner. This can be practised well before the flying change is asked for. Do this several times and your horse could well start to think as he nears the corner: 'Here we go again, another change of lead' – and he won't be surprised when eventually you ask him to make the change without first dropping to a walk"*. This is in stark contrast to many noteworthy trainers today who insist on jumbling many training elements into one and forcing the horse to do things instead of breaking them down and teaching him. So training becomes a patchwork of demands because there is no sequential aspect to the training programme. When horses take a long time to learn they will frequently get the blame rather than the trainer reflect on his lack of shaping. Modern day trainers would do well to heed Tom's words and those of behavioural science.

Cues and Signals

When we ride horses, we must remember that the signals and cues we give are our lines of communication. For optimal training, as well as for good welfare and common-sense the cues must be easily discriminated from each other by the horse. Tom was well aware of this and even prescribed different aids for each of the gaits: *"....it will be a great advantage if we can also clearly indicate to the horse as which of the three gaits we require him to go".*

Because the reins and legs initially reinforce certain movements of the horse's limbs, it makes sense to deliver the aids in accordance with when the limbs move and when they *can move*. For example, if we ask a horse to go and turn at the same time there will be confusion. However, if we ask the horse to turn as a foreleg is beginning to leave the ground, we can ask the horse to go immediately after because this is when the opposite hind leg is about to leave the ground. Recent work in neuroscience confirms that our optimum time to ask limbs to move is from the beginning and throughout the swing phase (i.e. when it's in the air). As soon as the leg is in the stance (ground) phase, other constraints such as balance and proprioception dominate the brain. He recognised the supreme but nowadays neglected horse training tenet that was established by François Baucher in the 19th century of *the independence of the aids.*

So many years after Tom's death, it now becomes clear why the aids should only be used in the swing phase and because the walk is the slowest of gaits, training the correct biomechanics is best done in the walk and then in the faster gaits; habits are already set so any mistakes in the timing of the rider will be less important. Tom knew of the supreme importance of the walk and declared that, *"The walk is known as 'the Mother of the paces'."* Considering the four beat gait of the walk and the facts just mentioned, it is therefore also necessary for the sake of clarity to separate the aids from each other because each leg beat in the walk has its own separate swing phase. Tom was correct to say: *"Remember, legs without hands and hands without legs. One must be passive while the other is active. This is applicable in all we are doing."*

Tom's initial background was with the Light Horse where he was heavily influenced by Captain J. J. Pearce. Captain Pearce instructed at the British Cavalry School at Weedon, whose very French influence goes back to Saumur before World War One. The Saumur Cavalry manual of Captain Pearce's time was very focussed on the concepts of François Baucher's "reins without legs and legs without reins" (independence of the aids). In other words, the separation of the aids which is not common today partly because of more recent German influences enabling a misunderstanding of Steinbrecht's classic text where he advised never to use rein aids without legs. What he most likely meant, was that when using the reins do not release leg *contact*, however he most likely did not mean to use a leg *pressure* at the same time! If he did then he was wrong.

This misinterpretation has dogged dressage theory ever since the rise of the German influence in dressage when they started beating the Swedes, who had a monopoly on dressage success for the majority of the 20th century. Germany's increasing dominance of dressage was powered by the sport's growing popularity. Post-war Western Germany became the breeding epicentre of dressage and jumping horses, producing up to 80,000 foals per year and providing the largest number of dressage judges at Olympic level. So it was not surprising that Austrian born Franz Mairinger was welcomed into Australia as our National Coach of dressage, which had slowly emerged as a discipline in the early 1950s. Franz, who had arrived in Australia as a post-war migrant, had a chance meeting with Tom who recognised the possibility that Franz was a man that could be of great importance in the future of Australian dressage. Franz Mairinger became a successful and perhaps Australia's most popular national coach.

To put things into perspective, some German equestrian history is important here. Unlike France and Sweden with centuries' old traditions in equitation, Germany's equestrian history is surprisingly recent and provincial. Germany as we know it, wasn't unified until 1871 and before that time, consisted of other regions including Prussia. The Prussian cavalry before the 19th century was strong, but in terms of horse training, no better than other European cavalries. Despite the popular view that the European cavalries were highly disciplined, scholarly literature tells a different story. There were many cases of horses running out of control through enemy lines, horses baulking, napping and running off. Of course we can't be critical of this because the horror of war is a nightmare and surely is a huge test for horses, and to habituate horses to all the sounds and sights of the darkest moments of war would be near impossible. It is not surprising that selective breeding for habituation abilities would be high on the agenda, and the Prussians were especially rigorous with the meticulousness of selective breeding. The heavy gun-carriage horses of Germany gave rise to modern German warmbloods, which is why in the period up to the 1990s the typical dressage horse was far less sensitive and less reactive than the thoroughbred, Arabian or Iberian horse.

In order to improve their military success, in the eighteenth century Prussia embarked on a mission to have better trained horses in the cavalry. Instrumental to this was E.F. Seidler who also had a military background, along with the riding master Louis Seegar and later on his pupil, the famous master horseman, Gustav Steinbrecht. These men introduced basic dressage principles to cavalry. Although many people think that dressage movements were designed for war, this is wrong.

Dressage and its high school airs were purely for entertainment in the royal courts of Europe while cavalry training was independently a very different matter. Seegar and Seidlitz were a formidable team. Seegar was a perfectionist in horse training and Seidler was a master at fixing behaviour problems. The precise effects of these men on the Prussian and then the German Cavalry are unclear; however, one thing stands out in the history of equitation – the Prussian cavalry rapidly became the most superior cavalry in Europe.

In terms of equitation, Steinbrecht's words are seen as providing the basis of the German system of horse training. Amongst his many credits, Steinbrecht is also understood to have promoted the idea that riders should never use hands without legs, so quite the opposite advice of the French trainer François Baucher who was famous for his doctrine of the independence of the aids. Steinbrecht's dictum pervades most German riding theory and is open to misinterpretation. And this is exactly what has happened. Ensuring that legs are used in conjunction with hands, as stated in the current German Federation Handbook of Riding may be interpreted as either: use *leg pressure* when using the reins or: maintain *leg contact* when using reins. The latter is correct in terms of animal cognition because the initial training of the horse involves very distinct operations of reins and legs: negative reinforcement of *deceleration* is provided by rein pressure, whereas negative reinforcement of *acceleration* is provided by leg pressure. So, obviously using the two together must involve some confusion; in behavioural science we know that individual animals vary in the way they deal with confusion ranging from active coping mechanisms to passive ones (so-called internalised stress).

Most German riding philosophies have misinterpreted Steinbrecht's dictum and believe that the rider should pressure with the legs when using the reins. This is the single most outstanding error of that system and it causes, in many individual horses, conflict behaviours. If the rider is adept at riding these conflict behaviours, apathetic passive coping mechanisms can give the outward appearance that all is well.

The reason I am pointing this out is that this is the conundrum that Tom faced when getting to understand the German training system that Franz Mairinger espoused. Tom greatly appreciated what he learned from his friend Franz. Indeed, the German concepts of losgelassenheit (looseness), durchlässigkeit (throughness and suppleness) and überstreichen (releasing reins to test self-carriage) provide important training goals. However, the use of simultaneous multiple aids did clash with some of Tom's knowledge that was hitherto so prescriptive and clear from his days in the Light Horse, coupled with his deeper learning from Captain Pearce and the British cavalry school of the time that had the strong French influence of Saumur and James Fillis (one aid at a time). One gets the sense in Tom's writing, especially in his final two books written in the 1980s that he was torn between his old French based philosophies and the German insistence of combined aids. Although Tom espouses Franz's beliefs about 'supporting the reins with the leg' and the supremacy of the leg aids over the rein aids, he isn't really committed to it because his emphasis on the importance of the uniqueness of the rein and legs aids shines through.

'Horse Control and The Rider' (1980) bears testimony to this odd mixture of equestrian ideologies. For example, he explains that: *"Leg aids must predominate – always, and their use must always precede the rein aids even when riding into a halt or a rein-back."* Later he advises: *"As his training progresses, the young horse comes to recognise that although a tightening of one rein means 'check pace and turn this way', the use of the rider's legs at the same time is meant to counter this stopping effect. He has to begin to weigh the effects of one aid against the other, and this weighting of one aid against the other becomes more and more important as training goes on"*.

In many respects, and probably unsurprisingly, it seems that Tom feared there was something he didn't understand about dressage so to appease his mentor and his readers, he chooses to accommodate the use of reins in conjunction with leg aids. In his heart I sense he always believed that when leg aids are used, the rein should be maintained at contact level (neutral) and when rein aids are used, leg aids should be maintained at contact level. When all of his early years are considered, the weight of the French influence and of his own sentiments and logic, I think combining the aids sat uncomfortably with him.

If only he knew that this was most likely a major misinterpretation and a travesty of animal training principles... Yet the relationship he had with Franz was a solid friendship and they shared a deep mutual respect. It is interesting to note however, in Tom's books after the 1970s, the diminishing clarity and prescriptiveness of his training advice as a result of the modern German influence. The indirect rein and the indirect turn, so pivotal in the French system from Saumur that informed the early British cavalry school, were absent in Tom's post 1970s texts as they are indeed absent in the modern German training system.

In a personal letter Tom wrote to the editor of the *Hoofs & Horns* in 1972, we can discern evidence perhaps of Tom's difficulty with Germanic dressage techniques.

"Do you know – Dressage has mucked up a lot of good horsemen. They start off with something that is successful. They are proving themselves to be tops. Then someone comes along and tries to teach them dressage. Or in the name of something else tries to teach them something. Wants to improve them. Wants to alter or change the method that he has been born with and sets him thinking and criticising himself and he, – Falls between the two stools."

Self-Carriage

I often say to people, "When you have trained a bird to sit on your arm, you need to let go of its wings in order to prove this training". If you can't do this because of fear of the bird flying off, then you can't claim to have trained it. The same is true for the horse's movement. The horse should be trained to self-maintain his own speed, straightness and outline. If the rider has to hold his outline or speed, or if one leg or rein has to be tighter to hold him straight, or if one leg or rein needs to act as a guarding leg or rein, then there is no self-carriage. This concept is true in all gaits. Even in the gallop, if the reins are released, or the legs are taken away from the horse's sides, he should keep his speed and line.

Self-carriage isn't just about making it easy for the rider, it is more essentially important for the horse's mental well-being. It gives the horse what we call in behavioural science predictability and controllability and through that comes mental security. The horse needs to feel free. Tom explained that: *"I should stress however that even when on a completely loose rein, our horse has to maintain both the direction and the pace he was working at when the rider dropped the reins".* Even at halt Tom warned: *"Note (my) words: He shall stand still, not he shall be held still".*

Short Sessions And Rests

Throughout his writing, Tom always maintained not only the importance of gradually building behaviours, but to do so in short training sessions interspersed with rest. When arousal levels go beyond the horse's sensibility, knowing when to rest is essential and this was well understood by Tom. He called this 'cup of tea time'. In the same way that physical fitness can be rapidly enhanced by interval training (short sharp, targeted bursts of activity with short rest periods in between), learning is also enhanced by the same approach. Experimental psychology reveals that training the horse in sets of repetitions, known as 'distributed practice' is more efficient than training in one single long session, known as 'massed practice'. Tom emphasised his 'End of lesson' concept where the horse would be rested as soon as it gave a correct responses or a series of correct responses: *"End of lesson – making a break in a lesson, pausing during a lesson, terminating a lesson – issued to encourage a horse to repeat what he last did before the break. As the horse's training progresses and we consistently utilise this to encourage him, he comes to watch for every little concession we make. Every pause or interruption becomes an encouragement."*

Flight Response

Horses are naturally sensitive and vigilant and tend to have a strong flight response. Animals such as horses that evolved in the open grassland habitat face the problem of always being under the gaze of the predator, so they need acute senses and a trigger-happy flight response. This response is very hard-wired and although selective breeding has dulled the flight response in some breeds, it is still there in almost all individuals, the difference being the eliciting threshold. The flight response is also more likely in horses with poor or unconsolidated training. Tom emphasised that the cavalry would never accept horses below the age of five years because they could not be relied upon either physically or mentally.

What we know about the flight response in terms of the way animals like horses acquire it, is that it is not a fixed, hard-wired response but is subject to learning. Tom was well aware of this in that he recognised that a well-trained horse with a strong flight response could be trained to be calm in difficult circumstances due to its higher level of internal security that comes from clear training whereas a horse with a naturally lower level of flight response could be made nervous through bad training. Poor training renders horses very insecure. In other words, an obedient horse is always quiet but a quiet horse isn't always obedient: *"...quiet horses have to be given all the preparation that more difficult horses need".*

Two things actually reinforce the acquisition of the flight response: how fast the legs move and how far they move. In other words, if something makes the horse suddenly veer sideways, known as shying, then how fast and how far he goes will determine the likelihood of the next occurrence of shying to that stimulus or something like it. Rather than ride through a dose of flight response, Tom was an advocate of slowing the horse or doing downward transitions to regain control of the horse's legs and to 'cancel' the incorrect behaviour and immediately replace it with a desirable one. He advised that when the horse gave an incorrect accelerating response: *"Try to tell him through the reins, and gently as always: 'Not that, boy; try again'."*

Tom also recognised that fear in people often resulted in anger which needs to be controlled, so that it never results in what he called *"uncontrolled brutality"*. *"Do all you can,"* he insisted, *"to control yourself"* and then *"the difficult horse will start to behave better".*

Arousal And Fear

The term arousal level refers to various stress levels that range from relaxation through to fear and includes the effects of various emotions and sexual arousal. It is measured by the effects of the hypothalamus and adrenal glands on the animal's body. Fear is clearly part of this continuum.

Alterations in the horse's fear and arousal levels can occur easily as the animal evolved in open grassland in full view of predators. Normally, however, horses can escape and can perfect their escape routines to solve these problems. When humans have horses on the end of the lead-rein or under-saddle this becomes much more complex because the horse is inevitably subject to competing and sometimes conflicting influences. In the wild, the horse is free to run or fight and thus respond to his environment in a biologically relevant way. However, if he runs when led or ridden for example, the competent handler or rider can slow or stop him, and any other anti-predator reaction can also be either prevented or thwarted. Although many horse people believe the opposite is true, the fact is that running away or shying sideways turns into a habit as result of two things: how fast he runs and how far. Sometimes of course the horse is too overwhelmed to stop straight away and that is okay; however it is a sensible idea to stop him where he can manage to calm down. Real calmness is achieved when the horse self-maintains his own rhythm – there are no random accelerations.

Arousal levels frequently rise in training. This can be largely unavoidable, especially if the task is physically difficult or unclear. Shaping is important so that any loss of clarity can at least be minimised. It is an important equitation science principle that arousal levels be kept low enough for the horse to still be able to learn and offer a response from a range of possibilities. What we see with persistently high arousal levels, is that the horse ceases to trial possible alternative solutions anymore, but instead his hard-wired fearful attempts to escape the stressful situation show up as tension, jogging etc. High arousal levels have been well documented to have an adverse effect on learning as Tom so rightly pointed out: *"...keep in mind that the horse must be calm to learn any lesson."*

The domestic horse also faces many environmental challenges that it is not naturally mentally equipped for, so it must habituate to the sight of dogs running about, plastic bags flying past, traffic and small children on bicycles rushing past. If the handler uses a careful desensitisation programme, the horse may well habituate. Tom pointed out that certain natural conditions such as windy days and moving objects also affect horses. He advised that riders, especially of young horses, should take this into account: *"A very windy day is a lost day with a young horse, as you will find it very difficult to hold his attention"*.

There is another side to this story of the horse's fear responses. The more confused the horse is about his training because the trainer has more than one pressure on simultaneously i.e. he applies rein and leg simultaneously, he drives the horse with his leg aids into strong and relentless mouth pressure, his signals are indistinguishable from each other, he doesn't shape responses sensibly or he uses the same cues for different responses, the more the horse may become frightened of new things, a state that scientists refer to as neophobic.

Few people recognise that confusion may well be the chief reason that the horse is neophobic, (frightened of things he hasn't seen before) and that this can cause him to be more afraid of new things in his surroundings. Indeed, even things that the horse was originally comfortable with may now cause it to become tense and shy or run. Confusion, because of its deteriorating effects on predictability and controllability, increases an animal's insecurity. So in addition to the hyper-reactive behaviours, confused animals also show increases in separation anxiety, fence walking and are more prone to stereotypical behaviours such as weaving and crib-biting. Tom was well aware of keeping the arousal levels low enough for the horse to learn: *"… if he is of a nervous disposition, move quietly around him until he calms down. If the surroundings of the yard are strange, let him have a good look around first. The calmer he is, the easier he will learn – ALWAYS REMEMBER THAT."*

While losses of control over the horse's own freedom can escalate the horse's coping mechanisms leading to increased hyper-reactivity, a competent handler or rider can still quash the horse's wildest reactions. With no recourse for escaping the stressful situation, the horse may now fall into a state of passive coping where instead of having raised heart-rate, blood pressure and vigilance, he now shows lowered heart-rate, lowered blood pressure and decreased vigilance. He has gone some way to 'shutting down'.

Shutting down (learned helplessness and apathy) however isn't an all-or-nothing state, it is a continuum. A horse can have learned to be almost entirely insensitive to the rider's spurs, which of course wouldn't have been the case when the horse was first started, yet other reactions to the rider may seem to be as available as before. His mouth may also be deadened to the effects of bit pressure, which again would not have been the case in his early days, yet other aids may continue to elicit good responses. (Full-blown learned helplessness occurs when the animal ceases to respond to any cue and fails to learn new ones.) When full-blown learned helplessness occurs the horse no longer reacts to any of the rider's signals.

Tom was careful to point out that training the horse needed careful management and that some horses would seem lifeless in the wrong hands. He was aware that consistent clear training so that aids were meaningful and unique and the horse was light to hand and leg was the way to avoid the myriad mal effects of stressing horses in training. Tom emphasised, "With how little force can we control our horse? Note the question is 'how little', not 'how much'." He explained that *"The better the horseman and the better trained his horse, the lighter will be the contact and the lighter the aids."*

Through examining Tom's life and his body of work there can be no doubt that he was a man who offered much during his life to the horses and humans within his sphere of influence. The following quote from his gravestone bears testament to the recognition that his work was significant and it has persisted beyond his lifetime.

> *"The greatest use of life is to spend it for something that will outlast it."*

> William James, Psychologist, Philosopher, Author – from Tom Roberts' gravestone.

Pat Roberts with author Andrew McLean.

Tom Roberts Legacy Project

It has been a true community effort to bring this story about the contribution of horseman Tom Roberts to the horse owners of South Australia and much further afield. There have been many individuals sponsor work, along with a crowdfunding page. Further information about supporters, contributors and the future aims of the project can be found on www.tomroberts.net.au

Insights from two of our largest contributors to this project:

SA Arabs Inc has sponsored this book out of the club's respect for Tom Roberts. Throughout his travels, Tom had a great deal to do with Arabians in both the Middle East and India. At the many training schools he conducted, Tom worked with numerous Arabians and part Arabians and admired their intelligence and sensitivity, his methods enabling their owners to achieve great success.

Carolyn Potts, Secretary, South Australian Arabian
Riders and Breeders Inc.

I was a new member of Horse Owners of the Southern Mt Lofty Ranges Inc. (HOSMLR) when I first met Tom. He was in a wheelchair then but still gave lessons and continued to pass on his knowledge to many riders. After his death Pat continued his work by distributing his books and donating sets of them to many groups and clubs over many years. Countless riders learnt to train their young horses by reading and learning Tom Robert's methods in easy to read and easy to understand language. We at HOSMLR are pleased to contribute to the legacy of republishing Tom's work in the new book to continue to help young riders train their horses in a kind and understanding manner which benefits all horses now and in many years to come.

Kay Scarborough, Secretary/Treasurer, HOSMLR

If you would like to contribute to future efforts to preserve Tom Roberts' body of work, e.g. film conservation, audio books and storage of artifacts, Horse SA has a budget line for this work.

Visit www.tomroberts.net.au or www.horsesa.asn.au for information on how to contribute to this project or email horsesa@horsesa.asn.au

Your anticipated support is greatly appreciated.

Tom presenting the Helen Junge Memorial Trophy to Louise Whibley.

Milton Keynes UK
Ingram Content Group UK Ltd.
UKHW021314071123
432132UK00024B/1190

9 780994 572134